As a Man Speaks,

... so it is.

As a Man Speaks,

... so it is.

Published by:

Hit Products
La Mesa, CA.

Where Ideas become Stars ☆☆

As a Man Speaks, so it is.
© 2020. Vic Van Maren Jr.
Edited by: Kimberly Knox

All rights reserved. This book may not be reproduced in whole or in part, or transmitted in any form, without written permission from the author or publisher except by a reviewer who may quote brief passages in a review, nor may any part of this book be reproduced, stored in a retrieval system, or transmitted in any form or by any means electronic, mechanical, photocopying, recording or other, without written permission from the author or publisher.

First Edition: March 2020.   10 9 8 7 6 5 4 3 2 1

Printed in the United States of America

ISBN#: 978-0-9836437-6-0

"Life is a Joyous Adventure. The Only Uncertainty is How Good it's Going to Be."

≈ ≈ ≈ © Tom Kelly

Acknowledgements

I owe a debt of gratitude to Kimberley Knox for her untiring work in editing this manuscript. Her willingness to grapple with these esoteric and sometimes mystical premises allowed me to continue in my attempts to make it clearer. Her kindly suggestions caused me to dig deeper,

Table of Contents

Introduction	11
Forward	14
Something for Nothing A Book and a Box	15
Cause and effect.	17
A Walkabout.	21
Chapter One. "As a Man Speaks, so it is."	23
Chapter Two. The Slippery Slide	29
Chapter Three. The Brief Recovery	33
Chapter Four. Tumbling Down	37
Chapter Five. Dealing with it	41
Chapter Six. The Cause and the Cure	45
Chapter Seven. Transformational Power & Trivia	49
Chapter Eight. Walking the Walk	53
Chapter Nine. Thought Control vs Peeling the Onion	57
Chapter Ten. The Weight of a Thought	65
Chapter Eleven. Victims of the Voice	69
Chapter Twelve. Is this Something Real?	73
Chapter Thirteen. What is This Something?	81
Chapter Fourteen. Your True Choice	85
Chapter Fifteen. Another Walkabout	91
Chapter Sixteen. The Moment of Now	95
Chapter Seventeen. Small Bites	99
Chapter Eighteen. Distinctions	101
Chapter Nineteen. They' Say Becomes 'You' say	107
Chapter Twenty. The Power of Listening	111
Chapter Twenty One. Point of View	115
Chapter Twenty Two. Things vs. Context	125
Chapter Twenty Three. Agreement	135
Chapter Twenty Four. Unconscious Choices	141
Chapter Twenty Five. The Power of Choice	147
Chapter Twenty Six. Affirmations and Assertions	159
Chapter Twenty Seven. Fear of Mental Chatter	161

Chapter Twenty Eight. Change,	
Identity Crisis vs. Shift.	171
Chapter Twenty Nine. Doing Time	177
Chapter Thirty. Something into Nothing.	
Nothing into Something.	183
Chapter Thirty One. Applying my Discovery	189
Chapter Thirty Two. Would you Believe?	193
Chapter Thirty Three. Where is What is Missing?	197
Chapter Thirty Four. The How to Use the Box	205
Chapter Thirty Five. A Few Bonuses.	
The Games of Empowerment	211

Introduction

My main purpose in creating this book is to give you back access to something you unknowingly gave away. This is something that over time slowly morphed into something you don't even know you don't know is missing. In simple terms, you just forgot. This Book and a Box is like a memory jog--a reminder of what once was. It has the ingredients of a mystery with a bit of drama thrown in. It contains numerous pieces of a puzzle and most of all a treasure map to guide those of you who are searching for the something that is missing in your life.

I too ,have experienced this tragedy, this loss, so if you will allow me I will begin by saying; "I hear you, I have felt your loss, your pain, and the words encased in this book will assist you in discovering and regaining possession of that something."

I have spent the better part of my life in search of this something while others seemed to carry on with the routine business of their lives. My life was like a mystery, yet as I worked, played, listened, read , studied, I was always on the look out, listening for a clue as to what this missing something was. What had disappeared? I longed for it, missed its presence, still I did not know what was missing. Glimpses came, always illusive, always just out of my reach, until one day I sat down at my Mac began to develop the focus it takes to write about something, this something that was missing in my life. Izy my spirit-muse showed up once in awhile until finally becoming a major part in guiding me to my discoveries.

As I began to write I started to experience the presence of this something, as it briefly stopped by for a visit when I would write, offering always a voice of encouragement. As I began to become more comfortable, more familiar with this unknown presence, it began to appear more often. Over time, as the blank pages filled with text, this something suddenly, yet quietly, appeared to be recognized. I felt its intent, its sincerity, its power. It was my voice, that voice I unknowingly gave away, , which I speak of throughout this book. It was the power contained within this voice—my voice--that had been missing in my life and this voice was presenting me with a choice.

Appearing only in thought form, being centered and assured, it spoke to me directly: "Take it or leave it. It is totally up to you," While being aware of this moment of recognition and choice I willingly appropriated my voice, causing an instant shift in my psyche and my core, the view of myself suddenly shifted from being powerless to having power. Much to my amazement I could now see myself, my life from a different point of view. In that moment in time I was out of my mind looking back, seeing the subjugated box I again had been living in.

At once, I remembered the loss of my power of choice, of my beliefs, and of the courage it had taken me to be true to myself when I was up against opposing forces plotting against this choice. I was again present to the choice of believing, the memory of the possibility of being able to transform past and present issues. To address thoughts, circumstances, issues, traumas, uncontrollable feelings, meanings, beliefs, and past hurts and turn them into the illusions they were with the least amount of effort. I needed to learn that it was again possible to have them transform--even to disappear.

Before you continue reading I want to clear up a few things first.

This is not a book that is leisurely read. It is not a bedtime story. It will require focus, brainpower, effort, patience and grit to get through to the end. You will actually have to study, do the work if you want the results I say are possible. I suggest you read it with a clear head, read it in small bites, and think about what I discovered and see how you can apply it to your own life.

Please give the following metaphor some thought, as it will assist you immensely in receiving the value I am placing in front of you now/

Picture in your mind an elephant. Now for a question. How do you eat an elephant? If you try and eat this book in one bite, you will feel overwhelmed, and maybe even a little confused and sick. If you become a bit kinder to yourself, just a little more forgiving, and be somewhat patient with yourself by studying and practicing the partaking of eating and digesting one bite of the elephant at a time, you will receive subtle insights of knowledge each time you apply what I assert as a possible truth I have discovered.

Whatever you do, do not let me lead you down any slippery slopes of instant millions; that is not my intention. Thinking for yourself since the time you have forgotten your something is difficult, sometimes hard, yet I have found the effort to be immensely rewarding.

A lot of us have already gone down paths by listening to those who would lead us down blind alleys created for their personal gain. I am not against personal gain, but what I am here for is being committed to giving you back the power and control over your life with the least amount of effort.

When I had the opportunity to do the est. training in 1975 I experienced something that produced amazing results, so I want to offer this suggestion: Life has rules and agreements. When you follow the rules and keep the agreements, this seems to create amazing results not available by doing your own thing. I ask you to agree to the following agreements; as they will assist you in getting the most value;

   1) Be conscious, alert and awake. Again, this is not a bedtime story. It is about your life, your past, present and you can be alone, completely involved in the ideas and words I present.

   2) notably your future. Make a conscious choice to read when Take the time to reflect on how certain chapters apply to your life.

   3) Read slowly ... think about the different ideas and

words, invite them into your life, and allow the ideas to enter your consciousness, allowing them to trigger memories or thoughts.

4) Do not pass by some word or phrase that you do not understand. Use the Internet or a dictionary to look it up. Get clear before continuing on.

5) Give yourself permission to think a little differently.

6) Get ready to face the possibility that at times you may feel confused, maybe even angry or upset. Tears may come, feelings from the past may surface to be recognized and addressed. Being frustrated at times is normal. This is leading edge thinking.

Now that we have covered the agreements, let me suggest another way to receive the most value. Attempt to stay present in each moment as you read--as the thoughts of your past, in love with attention and control, will visit often. Of this I am absolutely certain.

Something for Nothing

A BOOK and a BOX

The 'Crib Notes' version of the directions of how to get the most value from a self-help book (for the most part, mostly tried and failed) would go something like this:

1) Noticing or become aware of something you do not want. It might be a thought, a habit, a feeling, a belief, a person, or a thing.
2) Try and change it into something you do want = positive thinking,
3) Fighting it, argue with it. Resisting it with all your might.
4) Denying it is there.
5) Not thinking about it, demanding it not to be there.
6) Getting angry at it,
7) Bargaining with it.
8) Blaming others, blaming our parents, blaming yourself for it being there.
9) Feeling helpless in regards to handling it, calling people and ask for advice, hoping it will help.

10) Looking in all the wrong places for answers.
11) Thinking others know how to help you.
12) Deny feeling what you are feeling or try to not think what you are thinking.
13) Thinking no one would miss me if gone, thoughts of having no worth, because you can't change what is or what was. etc.
14) Placing post it notes or sticky notes on the mirror, steering wheel, office desk, iphone, anywhere you usually look.
15) Begging for relief.

*** All of the previous thoughts, beliefs, habits, memories, feelings, and actions come from the past, causing you to be at the effect (used by) of what was and is now.

Being willing to entertain the possibility, admitting to yourself, that you live within this unseen subjugated box (at the effect of) makes available the power to set yourself free from it's control over your life. Regaining the power to actually make the walls of the unseen box disappear, again allowing miracles to appear in your life.

"It ain't what you don't know that gets you into trouble. It's what you know for sure that just ain't so." © Mark Twain

Cause and Effect

"Shallow men believe in luck. Strong men believe in cause and effect." © Ralph Waldo Emerson

Cause and effect: In my opinion, this is the most powerful discovery known to man. Known is the word I chose, and for a reason. Man has known, has studied and continues to examine the results of cause and effect. These studies are still being used to sell us on the illusion of being powerless over our own lives. We are left being searchers of answers, chasing possessors of secrets and systems.
We pursue systems of getting this or that to occur (always in the future) to make us happy, content and at peace. This, of course, is insanity.
Everything is here right now and there is, but one something that is missing and that something is nothing, and everything comes from nothing.
Fundamental assumption: People are the sum total of what they believe. What causes beliefs? The 'language' of others, and the interpretations or 'meanings' given to the personal experiences we are 'subject to' within our surroundings. The

language of the collective unconscious we are immersed in and the meanings of experiences established brain patterns in our thinking minds early in life such that they are now habitual. We are at the effect or 'subject to' language, beliefs and meanings stated by the collective unconscious, ultimately create our point of view or understanding. As we grow older some of these beliefs are challenged by direct experiences and we discover that the language, beliefs and meanings we were subject to does not support who we are or who we choose to become. With various degrees of direct experiences beliefs and meanings, we are then able to transform them with the use of language, generating far more satisfactory results. What is possible is discovering the power within the language of beliefs with transformed meanings becoming the cause of knowledge and experiences. This insight shifts our point of view from being subject to (at the effect) of others language, beliefs and meanings (powerless) to being (at cause) of our own language, beliefs and meanings (powerful).

If you take a moment to look around and remember those past attempts to alter some thing you did not want to have in your life, you will notice that there are seldom any immediate or lasting results without an arduous amount of effort on your part. There is something missing--and this book is about what I discovered with regard to what I call that something.

Below is a quote that will assist you in getting the most value from this Book and a Box. This something, when utilized specifically, will produce results that will leave you amazed as to the simplicity of it.

"Have you ever noticed that when you choose to look at something differently, the something you are looking at changes?" This is a paraphrase of Werner Heisenberg's famous Uncertainty Principle.

When the above concept is experienced, it has within it the power to make things appear, disappear, or transform. I will explain the audacity—and the simplicity of that statement in the following chapters.

This concept will begin to show you how to speak to your own unconscious mind--the higher self or that part of you that mostly remains unheard or unseen by you. Entertaining the idea that it is possible that there is something you don't even know that you don't know--similar to a blind spot, accesses it. This is an invitation for you to choose to invite these ideas into your life for a brief visit—or get comfortable and stay. I ask that you entertain these ideas by focusing your attention on them, as you might do if you invited a good friend over for dinner or sat with them for a time to watch an enticing movie, or the mesmeric flames in a fireplace.

Allow yourself the pleasure of blocking out or letting go of the world and all its problems and just be with the potential value of these ideas. Set aside some time to step into the thoughts of discovery and maybe even experience a little intimacy with these moments. New, dreamy yet clear ideas will take you on a ride, an adventure of discovery if you just let go and trust them. You have total control, so at any time you can tell these ideas to leave should they become uncomfortable. One of the things I have discovered about the unconscious mind is that it fears specificity and being specific allows information to be transferred from one to another with the least amount of effort. This will become clear as you begin to embrace some of the principles I discovered.

A Walkabout

I want to take you through different stories, by way of an occasional 'walkabout' once in awhile threw out this book. This is a journey still practiced today day by the ancient aboriginal peoples deep in Australia. It is a right of passage in Australian Aboriginal, during which males undergo a journey during adolescence, typically ages 10 to 16 and live in the wilderness for a period as long as six months to make the spiritual and traditional transition into manhood. In a walkabout a mystical adventure is embarked upon in a quest to experience something called a 'blind spot within.' It is sometimes revealed, making way for true discoveries.

Ideas are intentionally repeated throughout this book to help you get from 'talking the talk' to 'walking the walk'. Talking the talk and walking the walk are distinct, in that talking the talk is not much more than mimicry, where as walking the walk opens our minds up to experiencing what is otherwise not known. Distinctions have within them tremendous value when utilized and internalized as they contain the seeds of growth and a state of being in action.

I will also discuss these phenomena you may have called; an 'identity crisis,' and the less well-known, but far more important, 'identity shift.' These are essential parts of being willing to let go of what you think you know. From there, this process allows you to entertain the possibility of getting a glimpse of this powerful unknown or undiscovered part of yourself. An example of this would be a term such as 'thinking outside the box' altered slightly to 'thinking from outside the box.' Adding one word alters your point of view, as I will also explain in a following chapter.

As I mentioned earlier, sticky notes are one of the ways we attempt to alter unwanted habits, things or beliefs we want to change within ourselves. I still use them occasionally as reminders to myself to pick up that quart of milk, yet as I looked back I noticed that when I used them to alter a behavior within, I was often left with a sense of frustration. I seldom experienced the changes I intended.

As I questioned and challenged the workability of various previously known and followed practices to alter behaviors, I finally had an alluring glimpse of that missing something. Thoughts were not enough, sticky notes fell short of the mark and even the practice of self-programming failed over time. Within this discovery I finally began to experience what worked and what didn't, and I began to sense that I was tantalizingly close to uncovering something new. There was this something I did not even know I did not know was missing.

Prior to writing this next paragraph, I did a short study on the nature of people. The results were amazing to me: as 60% said they would go to the end and read the instructions first. Are we really that impatient?

The directions of 'How to use this Book and a Box' are contained in the last chapters. But first I ask you to please read the book completely before discovering the How to. Why?

When you first look through a kaleidoscope you see one of its many possible facets. Here, each chapter is a facet, a look at yourself and the Box from a different point of view. Once you have read all the chapters you will have been given an enticing glimpse of your true power and potential and you will be able to see yourself and the Box in all its power. In time you will be ready to let go of the pursuit of understanding and you will know the value of letting go of being right. You will be able to experience what I assert is possible. With practice, you will become the viewer and the kaleidoscope.

Please read this book through one time and after you read the 'How to Use the Box', read it again. This is when you will remember and be able to trust the treasure map's guidance in leading you to the discovery of that something. The mystery will be solved, pieces of the puzzle will all fit together and complete the picture, allowing you to view the various facets displayed within the kaleidoscope called your life.

Chapter One

As a Man Speaks, so it is.

From my endless search for meaning, control and power over my own life, comes this offering for your inquiry and consideration. From the generously abundant moments I have experienced over my 79 years of life I have personally mined and processed the ore of numerous insights that have allowed me to discover something that, as the title above suggests, runs contrary to main line thinking.

It states that your voice has the power to produce amazing results. From the plethora of those direct experiments, those of discovering times I was not being true to myself, came insights and knowledge validating those moments, yet some of the reasons were still…unbeknownst to me hidden from my view. Eventually I discovered past programming based on the desire to look good, avoid looking bad, being right, avoiding being wrong and phrases like: "Sticks and stones can break your bones, but words will never hurt you." and "Opportunity only knocks once." I was left dodging sticks and stones and feeling angry because I missed my opportunity. All my efforts were focused on getting back what I already had been given whatever that was. Like peeling an onion, there were some tears to shed prior to getting to the core. As to mining and processing the ore, I began to mine the gold of experiences--encounters with people, and learning to mine for the gold within myself.

I rigorously tested various philosophies: metaphysics, ontology, cause and effect, various doctrines and both rhetoric and silver-tongued 'knowers'. Through these investigations I have discovered this truth for myself: Life itself has absolutely no one meaning. Our concepts of life have been made up, are being constructed, made up by billions of human beings around the planet, each of us after our own fashion, completely believing the messages that were programmed into their susceptible minds from birth and carried on into adulthood. There is no universal formula.

Indeed, there is a world outside of us. We can see and feel it as it compels us to conform to it, and to consume of it. We all have the freedom to resist it, rebel or petition against the way it is, embrace it or deny its existence. But being wired to habitually perceive everything as having meaning, we operate from the perspective of thinking, believing and acting on these meanings as if they are real.

We live a life at the effect of those meanings, believing that we are independent of them. Without those meanings living seems unbearable, so we desperately clutch onto the cause of our suffering. We are like the monkey—his hand full of candy in a jar—refuses to let go of anything, though he is trapped. Our hand clutches the means of freedom from inside the jar; we refuse to open our hand and let go of the meanings we have been told we need. Freedom from the habitual wiring and trapping of meanings allows you to be present, enabling you to finally live independent of meanings, and begin to live and begin to feel the joy of consciously giving meanings to life.

Most of the meanings, thoughts and beliefs we have about people are unconsciously repeated daily within relationships, groups and the workplace without any serious consideration as to whether or not they are even true. Like a statement spoken by Socrates. "The unexamined life is not worth living" changed the course of my life as I finally came to a place of being not only sick and tired, but also tired and sick of the language used by the collective unconscious.

The essence or core of what makes up a human being, what got us to where we are at the present time is mostly overlooked, unknown and ignored--beyond the grasp of our knowing or experiencing whilst we are shackled by programmed thinking. This practice of attempting to control thoughts, solidly programmed from our past has become futile. From inside this life of an illusionary box, it is difficult to see this as a true prison which we have chosen to live in...one to which we have allowed ourselves to be.

The main contradiction, expressed as a point of view, is concerning James Allen's book, "As a Man Thinketh". This is not an attack on his book, far from it, as much of the progress of society as a whole has come from us using this philosophy of thought being the *something* that would generate power, and control over one's life. For many years I too simply believed in the main premise of this little volume, the premise that man is literally *what he thinks,* his character being the complete sum of all his thoughts.

It wasn't until life served me notice with a disturbingly cunning and powerful wake-up call and began shaking me into conscious, proactive action that I began the arduous task of searching deeper within myself. It wasn't until I challenged myself to think beyond this given premise and question its validity and value in my own life, that insights began to appear. Much to my surprise these insights continued to appear as contradictions to this given premise of thoughts being all-powerful and controllable. As this slow tedious pace of acquiring meaning, control and power in my life by thought control continued to cause rapid stirrings of angst, and restlessness to repeatedly haunt my waking hours. I, like Alice in Wonderland was about to go:

Down
the
Rabbit Hole
in Search
of that Something

Having been self-employed for some 45 years as a general handyman and buying and selling at garage sales triggered the presumption of quid pro quo as it governed many of my experiences. Exchanging my time and energy for the almighty dollar was necessary to keep the boogeyman of survival at bay. Over those many years I became a combination of a treasure hunter, and a scientist of the mind as I searched for answers to the questions that permeated my relentless sense of inquiry.

The privilege of being self-employed allowed me the freedom to be exceedingly inquisitive with regard to extracting insights into new ways of generating ideas and producing results. I studied cause and effect, ontology, the laws of attraction and I even created four Magic Card Stories, each telling a different story. A Magicardstory™ is a story told by you and a deck of playing cards. Even though you have someone cut the cards 5 different times, the cards match the story as it unfolds, creating a ... Magical Illusion of the cards ... Appearing ... AS YOU SPEAK. They can be found at thebookpatch.com or amazon.com or barnesandnoble.com under my name and purchased.

These books I playfully created to hone my writing skills, while seeming innocent in the beginning, had within them secrets about life's mysteries, life's potential. Some years later my best friend in Louisiana emailed me a video he had copied off the internet. Much to my delight it was a video of Willie Nelson sitting across the table with a friend. He was performing a similar rendition of one of the Magic Card Stories I had created. I watched with breathtaking amazement as he turned over each card as he told the story. The reaction of his audience was, as I have experienced often, mesmerizing. Willie has always held a special place in my life, mostly as a role model of his carefree, gentle nature and alluring poise. I have always enjoyed his music and his acting, as he is a true American hero of mine.

Willie Nelson shares a card trick

This illusion of cards appear as one speaks, even when someone cuts them 5 different times, often shows up as entertainment in the moment for many, but for me it appeared as a glimpse of an innate gift I was given at birth. The ability, the power to have a say in the matter of my own life had somehow been undermined, overshadowed by the rhetoric of mental chatter of the past overriding common sense, that of being true to myself. I had allowed myself to be dumbed down, as I was confused and afraid, refusing to speak for myself. This search for something that could reverse this intentional overpowering, undermining destruction of my voice brought me close to an edge, close to the cliff of responsibility. You see, I took it very personal, as I did not enjoy the feelings of being held hostage by the 'gift' of language being used against me.

"Each man must look to himself to teach himself the meaning of life. It is not something discovered: it is something molded." © Antoine de Saint-Exupery.

Chapter Two

The Slippery Slide

    A few years later after I retired from my previous endeavors my interest turned to the Internet. I loved to sell on Ebay and Amazon, and this led me into a lucrative business of selling books on Amazon for 7 years, but in 2009 Amazon suddenly closed my account due to a grave misunderstanding which challenged my integrity and my security. For the next six months I tried hard to pretend that I didn't need Amazon to keep me busy after retirement and that losing the income didn't matter—Hah!
    I was totally traumatized and ended up spending another six months watching selective TV programs, trying not to experience those feelings and trying to stop the thoughts that were robbing me of the life I once knew. The more I tried to accept, ignore, fix or change what had happened the deeper down I slid into the abyss of meaning. I couldn't read, I couldn't watch any TV except Poker after Dark and The World Series of Poker. It was when I lost my confidence to drive that my desire to live slipped away taking me into the thoughts and feelings of helplessness. This combination of my thoughts being out of my control and experiencing feelings I did not understand had me close to the clutch of absolute despair.
    I finally called my doctor and he put me on meds to stem the intensity of the slide this change had triggered. It was early in November of 2010, while attempting to turn a single negative into a positive, which I told one of my daughters that I was going to do something special on my 70th birthday. Come to find out that the word 'special' can have very different meanings, and in late November I began to slide into a deep depression. I had

reached the end of my rope and what was below me was the fear of falling deeper into the unknown.

Both my daughters were there for me. Lori, my oldest, called me at least two times a day, drove me to my doctor's appointments when I no longer felt I was capable of driving, set up appointments for me, paid my bills and kept me aware of the meds I was taking. She even connected me with a support group where I met with people who faced similar challenges that were getting better.

Linda, my second daughter, invited me to my Grandkid's concerts and the San Diego Youth Symphony that allowed me to get my mind temporarily off my depression and decreased appetite. The peace I felt during that time allowed me the space to attempt to reconnect with my lost self.

My sister made herself available if I needed to talk, as did my sister-in-law Jackie, who was always there late at night just in case. A true friend in Louisiana told me to call him 24/7. I even had a good friend in Palm Desert who had already slid down a similar path that I called, hoping for some guidance. Still, I could not snap out of it. They had all done there very best to stop the slide I was on. I spent hours on the phone trying anything that was suggested.

The depression then manifested into feelings of anxiety, lasting for some 6 hours during the day, followed by the complete loss of appetite, the lack of feeling pleasurable feelings and finally a loss of interest in life. Fighting the battle I was facing and not gaining ground began to take its final toll. Suicidal thoughts began to crop up every so often, so I again went to see my doctor. After he suggested some different medications the anxiety somewhat subsided over time. I was fortunate enough to have a daughter who took my symptoms to heart and kept encouraging me to check myself into a hospital, as my suffering was neither normal nor necessary. So with trepidation and Lori at my side, I checked myself into a hospital and was diagnosed with GAD (General Anxiety Disorder) on December 17th.

"Wow! Is this where I am going to spend my 70th birthday?" I thought. Call it what you will, fate, chance, or destiny was in charge. I was not in charge and I knew it. I was lost in the confusion of thoughts and feelings I did not understand. I was lost and making world record time gathering up thoughts of confusion, doubt, fear and shame.

I spent 14 days (it rained 10 of those days) in the hospital. I missed the comforts of my home, yet oddly enough one of the things I missed the most was the pitter-patter rain makes on the aluminum window coverings on my house. I spent Christmas Day in the hospital instead of being at Linda's house with my family. Spending Christmas in the hospital was hard on all of us. We all missed our families, and
I missed the joy I felt when we are all together for those special moments. I was able to call Jackie almost every day for much needed support from someone I knew cared about me. Much to my surprise on Christmas afternoon my daughters Lori
Linda and Patrick, my Grandson showed up for a visit during my stay at the hospital. I was given gifts I had trouble understanding and accepting, let alone being comfortable with, as it was all about me. There were nurses every shift, 24 hours a day. There were mental health workers, a psychiatrist, and even a psychologist. The whole staff was there to check my heart rate, my blood, my sleeping patterns, my appetite, my bathroom habits and my social habits as well as a Clinical Director of Mood Disorders who I was able to talk to every day. There were also card games, craft classes, a pool table, a basketball court, a swimming pool and even a Jacuzzi to enjoy. I even started to attend classes for three or four hours during the day, learning cognitive thought exercises to keep my mind busy, which would turn out to be very valuable in my future.

The people I met at the hospital were wonderful. They encouraged me, supported me, cried with me and laughed with me. We became like a little family. Then, on my birthday, December 26th about 8:30pm I felt the emotions of being gutted like a fish. They gave me a card, and little presents they had made during the craft classes. Each person had signed the card with encouraging words of loving support. Tears came forth as I lost complete control as I began to feel the caring that was all around me. All these people gave me something I just could not see, let alone experience—hope for a future!

The overwhelming gift of caring touched me deeply on my

70th birthday. It was definitely something 'special' after all. I had received cards, kisses and hugs from total strangers going through their own trials and tribulations at the hospital. Some of those gifts I still carry with me today. At that very moment I knew it was exactly what I needed to snap out of it.

One of the things I learned came from my day nurse Mario, who told me, "My joy comes from the person who receives my gifts, in the simple form of a thank you. When it is not received I am robbed of that joy." So simple, yet it made so much sense.

Chapter Three

A Brief Recovery from the Slide

Now I needed to find within myself a way to get home. This cognitive therapy was the key and Izy, my spiritual muse was beginning to whisper in my ear again late at night. "You are getting better, so let's go. You know what to do. Let's get back on track, by speaking some new ideas." I thought more about writing as it was suggested as part of the process of getting stronger, so I began to journal again. Then I started to tell everyone that I was going home this year, like a joke, as it was just five days prior to New Year's Eve. I also told them I was going to spend the New Year practicing what I knew to be true, that of laying down some new verbal tracks so I could step into a new future. I wrote in my journal, pictured myself at home on my Mac writing.

My roommate Tim had set the example as he had gone home just a few days earlier. Here was a guy in a wheelchair who was completely functional with just one leg, being 100% responsible for his own independence. Looking back into my own past I think I took much of my independence for granted. I decided, no more! I watched Tim handle the endless paperwork and challenges that hindered his release with the wisdom and grace of a wise old soul. As I reflected on our conversations my light of hope for the future started to burn a little brighter. It was time to get to work and do what I knew worked for me. I got busy journaling, picturing and speaking, "I am going home on December 31st or sooner."

The very next morning, as I walked by the board where all of our names were listed, I saw "release" written by my name. Were they going to release me? No way! I instantly got hold of a nurse and asked why my name had a release by it. She told me that there was a refusal of insurance coverage pending. A problem with my insurance was more than I was able to handle, she knew it. Panic slipped in as I contemplated the outcome.

I had completely forgotten that I had been saying that I would be going home by the end of the year. Two hours later my doctor walked by. He was a man short in stature, yet tall in respect. "Let's talk," he said as though on a mission. He found a private room and invited me in for a chat. After a few pleasantries he got on the computer and looked again at all the information that had been collected over the past 10 days. "You are doing very well, your appetite has improved, and your sleep habits are much better. All your vital signs are good and you interact with people, go to the classes and participate more than most. Your meds have also stabilized you. Do you want to go home? I will release you if you think you can deal with life at home."

Surprisingly enough, I started to argue and said that my appetite had not yet returned completely, that I could never learn all the information presented in these classes, and that my insurance company was refusing to cover my stay. They thought I was well enough to handle everything on my own at home.

I will never forget his response. He started to laugh. He was laughing with me, not at me. He said, "Vic, you are doing a fantastic job here. No one could learn all the information presented here in just two weeks. That is not the intent. You can study at home and as far as your lack of appetite is concerned, you can eat what you like, it will return soon enough. As to the insurance company your social worker will handle the insurance company, don't worry about it." The very next day a social worker came to see me to file an appeal, and stop the forced release.

Laughter and tears came at the same time. For the first time in a long time I was acknowledged for doing a fantastic job, and given the assurance that a loss of appetite was not a terminal condition. As for the insurance thing well, it went 'poof,' into the never land of my mind. My doctor was a man I had grown to trust as he shot straight. He gave me a choice, the choice to either be a victim or to be at cause by being responsible for my own release.

Three days later the paperwork came for my release and I remembered what Tim's example had taught me and what Jackie, my sister-in-law, had told me many years ago. "Patience is a bitter cup, only the strong can drink." I would need that patience, that control of my thoughts and emotions as I began the journey though the rules and regulations toward release.

On December 31st Lori picked me up from the hospital just as I had spoken. We first drove by and picked up my meds then she drove me home. Once I was home the first thing I needed to do was get clear about my medicine. We both sat on the couch and I started to separate the bottles of pills and put them in their little compartments. She, being as she had been handling everything for me in the past 2 months, attempted to assist me. Just then, I felt something different. At first I did not know the feeling, yet I attempted to express it to her. "I saw myself doing this by myself, please understand. I need to do this, as it is very important. I need to know when to take the right meds at the right time." She just smiled and said, "No problem Dad, I want you to know." Then off she went with a hug and a huge thank you from a very grateful father.

After she left I began to search the Internet and began to read anything I could get my hands on, in an attempt of gaining enough knowledge and understanding to discover the meaning, the cause of my past experiences as I was now on a committed mission to find the cure.

Chapter Four
Tumbling Down

Being as Lori had found me the support that dealt with similar issues I continued attended each Saturday. Over the next 6 months the meds, the knowledge and experiences at the hospital gave me some needed relief as the anxiety and depression lifted a bit, leaving me giddy with relief. After some time had passed I felt somewhat normal again,
 arrived at a place where the thoughts of no longer needing to take the meds took over. Some lessons are difficult to learn, , I was about to learn the hard way. I stopped taking my meds without my doctor's knowledge.

Waiting for continuing signs of progress had often been a time to inform myself, attempting always to gain insights into progressing forward, so I begin to look for something of value to fill my days. Even though I felt better, time was still not on my side as I had too much of it to fill. The memories of the anxiety and depression still lingered, capturing a great deal of my thoughts, my attention.

It all began during one of those waiting times when I was teetered on the edge of boredom that I decided to look into Coda, Co-dependents Anonymous, thinking there might be some information that would assist me in finding the cause of this debilitating annoying reality. Being a self-discovery group that studied the effects of coming from a dysfunctional family unit, I saw that I fit into their criteria. I attended a few meeting and eventually looked at getting a sponsor to assist me on the path to freedom from some of the issues that still kept me from being fully expressed. As suggested, I listened for someone who had been in the program for a few years prior to making my choice. After some months I gathered up the courage to approach a person I thought might be of help in guiding me through the steps. He had attended the meetings for about three years, and had sponsored others.

As we attempted to set up a time to meet, I expressed to him that I was not much of a morning person, but his work schedule required us to meet in the morning so I agreed. I showed up early, which was normal for me and waited in the parking lot. He arrived right on time and we went inside and got seated in a booth, ordered some coffee and I attempted to strike up a conversation with him, asking him about his experiences with Coda.

I was not ready for what I received. He began with indignantly telling me that he was not going to pick up my shit or handle my issues as he had enough to deal with in his own life. My response irritated him even more as I expressed to him that I did not know how this program worked and I just need a little guidance. Little did I know I was sitting in a restaurant with a person who, unbeknownst to me, had just done a line of cocaine. I was emotionally open to his friendship by my own choice, yet I did not know he was using as he expressed himself at the meetings as being someone that had not used for two years.

The earlier effects of anxiety and depression had caused me to still be extremely vulnerable to outside stimulus, which he was aware of, so I thought I was safe in his presence and my protective guard was not up. Suddenly, out of nowhere came the effects of the drug he had been using transferred over to me, plummeting me into the effects of the drug he was on. When the rush of the drug entered my body I experienced a huge overload of adrenalin. Being as I was not a user of experimental drugs, this transferred overload shook the very core, and my body and my mind reacted to this by going straight to the fear of the unknown. The shock of this unknown feeling caused me to hyperventilate profusely, which instantly caused more fearful thoughts to overtake my reality.

Suddenly a full force panic attack surfaced, capturing the totality of my attention, morphing into the laser thought of breathing becoming my only thought. The panic of that abrupt alteration in my reality then caused me to bolt out of the restaurant thinking I could out run what had just happened, as I did not have the knowledge or experience to deal with it. If was as though some alien being had come crashing into my body, reversing all the poles of thought from positive to negative. Fear had raised its ugly head and I did not know how to handle it. Doubt, shame, anger, hate, resentment and guilt were all I heard, all I felt, causing my body to react, magnifying the fear. As I drove away that reaction plummeted me straight into the throws of victimhood.

When I returned home I had calmed down a bit, so I attempted to reflect on what has transpired. I was about to discover my lack of understanding had taken a terrible toll on my stability. I recognized this way of perceiving myself as a victim, as I had studied cause and effect for many years and had pulled myself out of similar perceptions. The numerous times prior to this, I was aware of the possibility of there being a cause. This was, as I was to discover, much different as it triggered memories from my past where I had run from this emotion of fear. It triggered within me that fight or flight response hidden deeply within us all.

Chapter Five

Dealing with it.

The idea of writing this Book and creating a Box began to crystalize out of necessity after I suffered that horrific panic attack that triggered the anxiety and the return of the debilitating depression. I was now face to face with a dilemma, the unwanted choice of returning to the hospital. It was then, as I mentally went back to my experiences and what I had learned over the two weeks in the hospital that I recalled my Doctor's last words to me. He actually wrote it on a prescription tablet for me to take home with me. The words: "Deal with it" were written in that scribble doctor's write, but I knew what it meant. That piece of paper represented something he saw in me, something I did not know I did not know about myself.

The doctor I saw at the hospital was semi-retired and only visited the hospitals on occasion, so I now needed to find a new Psychiatrist and fess up to the misjudgment of taking myself off my meds. What I came face to face with was my stubborn rebellious nature not to take the meds. I searched for a doc in my area and made an appointment. After coming clean about my mistake in judgment this new doctor's prognosis was not what I wanted to hear. Being told I would have to learn to deal with my disorder using drugs again, and that I would just have to learn to live with the anxiety didn't bring forth the happy camper in me. My stubbornness was not going to die a quiet death, as it was then that I made a life altering choice. I refused to accept having to learn to deal with and live with the prognosis, yet I agreed to accept the assistance of my newly discovered Psychiatrist. He asked me a few questions and suggested I start taking a well-known drug to deal with the anxiety and depression.

As I began my monthly sessions with the new Psychiatrist I entered the world of opinion and the secretive, often unspoken words of, 'I do not know'. Doctors are often portrayed as knowing, and act as if they know. It was an innocent mistake on my part, believing my doctor knew what meds would work in my body, yet I continued to trust his knowledge. When I experienced him changing the medications and the doses over time, it often left me feeling less than a person as his actions did not match what I believed. In the beginning this was a great affront to my newly discovered naïve belief--that of thinking that doctors knew more than they actually knew. I soon came to realize that this also came from the constant barrage of the media advertising that constantly repeated the phrase of "talk to your doctor" as they touted the next pill they were promoting. In the beginning when my friends asked about my progress, I often referred to him as being my drug dealer. Unbeknownst to me, I had allowed these sales pitches to undermine my own common sense.

After a few visits my daughter suggested that I should also contact a Psychologist to assist me in dealing with the consequences of the anxiety and taking the drugs again. I soon found a doctor close to my house. Over time she became someone I learned to trust, enabling me to discover and accept all the facets of what made me tick. She provided the space for the real me to reemerge as I received numerous insights into myself from her that I still use today.

I continued through the process of having my meds adjusted up and down and over time changed completely, as this doctor seemed to have various ideas as to what might work. I then settled into the newly unwanted routine of doctor's visits and reluctantly accepted the debilitating reality of being a guinea pig of discovery, that of the agonizing experiences of discovering what worked, and what didn't work. I just bit the bullet and accepted what I thought I could not change. I spent about a year with this Psychiatrist and received nothing but a ten-minute unproductive conversation of; "continue to take the prescribed pills". I soon reached that point of 'something has to give' and mentioned this plight to my daughter. Her reply was adamantly clear. "Dad, there is no reason for you suffering this amount of pain." The suggestion of finding a new Psychiatrist was instantly thrown into the mix. As soon as I took her advise I reached out and connected with a doctor with ethics.

On my first visit this new Psychiatrist sat with me and took the time to explain to me that my insurance had always authorized a 30-45 minute consultation. After I spent a few minutes feeling less than, for again allowing myself to be taken advantage of, I accepted his assistance and set up a monthly appointment.

On my second visit to my new doctor's office, there was now time to express my concerns, as I now had 30-45 minutes of his time. The time I had allowed myself to be conned out of over the past year was still fresh in my mind. "Stupid is, what stupid does" came to mind. Within ten minutes of being in his presence, I felt I had found a doctor current with the cutting edges of knowledge, yet this reality of looking to a doctor to know and not finding it was now staring directly back at me, and there was no sign that said; 'let's make a deal'. Believe me, I looked for one! It was what it was and dealing with it was now center stage. I came clean with my new doctor and voiced my concerns and my disappointments in regard to my past experiences and beliefs. His response was exactly what I needed to hear as he explained that yes, I was going to experience being a guinea pig of discovery as he really did not know what worked in my body. (Wow, honesty appeared and took a bow!)

He further explained to me that his job was to find out what worked in my body and he needed my help in finding this out. He simply explained the obvious, that being that each body reacts differently to different meds. Suddenly the role of guinea pig seems like it might be less that a chore. He stated that it might even be a learning experience for us both. It was then that the past experience of being taken advantage of lost its sting, and I suddenly opened up to the feeling of partnership he offered. It was exactly what I needed to feel.

Over time we tinkered with the meds as I desperately began to hold onto the assumptions of being told by him that I could possibly expect small traces of stability and control to re-appear over time. His words seemed to counter my fears when time began to slip into the enemy's camp of: I want results now. Thankfully, I had developed a strong constitution of patience over my years of being self-employed as I was about to be repeatedly tested as the conversations of required adjustments to my meds continued.

Over about two years he became a trusted ally and assisted me in getting completely free of the drugs, as I was still not to keen on the idea of having to use drugs as the fear of becoming dependent was still programmed into my mind. Even though I tried to resist the conversations of fear, they had dug themselves deep into my psyche and were ready and willing to challenge my choice, as they were in for the long haul.

Chapter Six

The Cause and the Cure

I will not go into the long details of the processes, trials and errors, blind alleys and false assumption I uncovered during this discovery of both the cause--and the cure--of the panic attack or the intense state of anxiety and depression. I will state what I finally did to reach beyond mere knowledge, and discover the something I knew was missing. The turning point is relevant, as it allows some insight or a view of the stand I had to take to align with the experience of 'knowing I knew'. I was about to discover something located within allusive direct experiences that would gradually reveal to me the privileged secret insights hidden in the powerful elixir of knowing that you know.

I had lived enough of life to recognize certain things about the nature of human beings regarding our patterns, beliefs and actions (including myself) and the one characteristic that seemed to surface more often than others was this thing called the search for knowledge and understanding.

Knowledge and understanding are great tools, yet when counted on as being sufficient within themselves, they can actually stifle one's stretch in revealing the secrets of real discoveries. It was while in this quandary of having gained a certain amount of knowledge and understanding that I discovered their limitations. There was repeatedly something missing in regard to the recognition and location of a cure and I intended to uncover this missing something. It was fairly easy to let go of thinking that I knew, as the obviousness of not knowing was very present, yet I was reluctantly willing to let go of the arrogance of being right and open up to what others thought was possible. As I repeatedly shoveled through the multiple well meanings, opinions and beliefs of others I began to peal away the layers of misinformation that hindered me from discovering this something beyond knowing, beyond understanding.

"If you leave the smallest corner of your head vacant for a moment, other people's opinions will rush in from all quarters. " © George Bernard Shaw.

I was aware of my explorative nature with regard to the hunt, the thrill of discovery, yet unaware of the skills required for an intensely focused desire to rid myself of this killer of my once experienced life. I was more than willing to stretch the boundaries of my thinking, basing it on the gift of fluid perception I used in my daily life. As I began this journey, searching for the knowledge wherin I could rid myself of this plight, one of my favorite sayings I repeated to anyone who asked about my plight was, "I will try anything. I will even try spreading peanut butter on wet bread." As to that silly saying, I was not consciously aware of the power that was contained within it, let alone that it was about to allow me to learn something that, over time became much more valuable than the knowledge and understanding I pursued. It opening me up to a source of knowledge that enabled me to discover the cause and finally experience the cure. Unbeknownst to me, discovering the cure was just the beginning of what this experience had to offer in regard to the value it contained.

Meds from my new Psychiatrist and counseling with my Psychologist had allowed me some needed relief from the depression, but the anxiety still governed most of my thoughts. Over the next six months I continued to go to the support group my daughter had found for me as it gave me something to fill my time and socialize once again. Everyone at the meeting was familiar with my story so I felt safe enough to share about my days being good or bad. This particular day I was feeling slightly on edge, somewhat anxious about my future and I mentioned this in passing during the meeting. After I expressed my concerns, a woman mentioned a class she had discovered that she thought might be of interest to me. I wrote down the information she provided, and when I returned home I looked for more information on the internet.

It was a class called Recovery International and it dealt with similar issues I was facing. The classes were free to attend and there were numerous meetings held on different days and nights. I found a schedule of the meetings and decided to give it a shot. I really had nothing to loose but time and I had an abundance of that commodity.

At the first meeting I became aware of two books. A Psychiatrist, Abraham Low, M.D. wrote them in regards to his discoveries and direct experiences with his patient's anxiety and depression over his many years of practice. His main interest became one of discovering why his patients would get well and then relapse. That one statement regarding relapse caught my attention as it aligned with my past experiences, my outrageous desire and my belief that there could be a possible cure. Strangely enough, these classes also aligned somewhat with the est. training I had done some 40 years earlier. I returned home, hit the internet and purchased both books. Upon the arrival of the two books I discovered Dr. Abraham Low, M.D. was indeed a Psychiatrist back in 1937, and he gave lectures regarding his discoveries. As I intently studied his works I discovered that his assertions aligned with my already internalized beliefs regarding the possibility of exposing the hiding place of this allusive cure. He agreed that it was possible and that was all I needed. Both of his books provided me with certain principles he had discovered while practicing his trade as a Psychiatrist. Over time I was able to grasp hold of his wisdom and as I internalize it. I began to experience the results he wrote about. No amount of praise would be enough to thank him for the taking of his time to give those lectures and to the Foundation of Recovery, Inc. for publishing his books: Mental Health Through Will-Training and Manage Your Fears, Manage you Anger. I owe both a great deal of gratitude.

Along with the support I received from my daughters,

sister-in-law and a few close friends, I began to gain some solidity by extensively feeding on Dr. Low's stated direct experiences and discoveries. It was not until I came up against resistance or lack of belief from others, as to the possibility of uncovering the cause and finding the cure that my previously unknown degree of unwillingness came into view. I immediately, relentlessly focused my mind on the wisdom he offered, , aiming it directly at myself. I diligently trained my mind to remember, to recall what happened prior to the event that caused the panic attack. I was then struck with an overload of incoming data from both of the following studied premises: Transformational Power (est) & Trivia (Recovery International).

"There is something I do not know, the knowing of which could change everything." © Werner Erhard

Chapter Seven

Big Words:
Transformational Power

Little Word, Great Power:
Trivia

The basic premise of the est training, which I had participated in during the early 70's, was that we are unaware of our own transformational powers. The basic premise of the current forum founded on Dr. Low's books, Recovery International, states that in order to progress we must learn to view and interact with life's events as trivialities.

These two concepts, Transformational Power and Trivia began to meet on equal ground and began forming an intimate relationship within my mind. Both had, over time, developed distinctly unique personalities of their own. What caught my attention was when this little seemingly unassuming entity called Trivia stepped forward intending to be heard.

As the trains of thought regarding transformation had often woven their way through my life, I began to experience whispers of power drifting in, triggering thoughts and memories of what once was. Then, without provocation this little entity called Trivia again requested the recognition of taking center stage as she was not to be dismissed.

As first Transformational Power thought less of this inferior little entity called Trivia. It was not until Trivia began to speak, gently pressing to be heard, that Transformational Power began to take notice of the something within the voice of this little unassuming entity. Being unaware of this power caught him off guard, as Trivia was calmly able to hold her ground.

There seemed to be something these two characters wanted me to witness so I would often, with a bit of perplexity, step back and intently listen. I was now privy to viewing Transformational Power and Trivia having intimate dialogues, which appeared on the movie screen of my mind. I was able to watch and listen as each made great strides in fully expressing their points of view. After many hours of these intensely informative discussions, I witnessed them come to a truce as they reached the balance of respect and friendship. Each had offered their personal unique value for me to consider, somehow leaving me with a calm feeling of balance.

This one simple little unassuming entity 'Trivia' spoke to me of containing enough power to give me back total control over my life over time through consciously and proactively choosing to practice and train myself.

Then, Transformational Power began to speak to me of the something I had been searching for and began to expound on the conversations he had with Trivia.

"Both of us came to the conclusion that we had many powerful traits in common. I had a past meaning, that of being aloof, a bit difficult to access. To be returned to the power I have always been I simply need to be recognized and appropriated. To live and become alive I need to be spoken from the space of 'nothing' or anew."

As he continued on "Trivia then spoke to me about her past meanings; that of being nothing, lacking in value. She spoke of the means of being returned to the power she still is. To live and become alive she too needs to be recognized and appropriated-- to be spoken anew, from nothing."

He then summarized. "We discovered our commonalities; that of both needing to be recognized and appropriated then spoken anew from 'nothing' to be returned to our true power."
Words, though just letters strung together, have within them the power to create realities within when joined together. Each one needs to be respected and recognized as having this power. The balance I was left with came from accepting the fact that Transformational Power and Trivia are equal in this power when viewed accordingly, just as Something and Nothing are the same with regard to power, as they are both inseparable and interchangeable.

I agree, these are bold statements, yet I can confirm that these statements are not only factual, but also possible as they are based on a great number of direct personal experiences. When used correctly with the directions in this book you will gain the ability to experience exactly what I am stating.

Now, let's see if I can place the correct words on paper to

entice you into accepting this as fact, therefore allowing you to apply and act on what I have discovered.

If you are like most of the population that feels overpowered by the bombardment of so-called truths and secrets, you have acquired this book attempting to discover the answers to those mysteries or riddles. This is a book that will deliver on its statements. I can at least guarantee you this one fact: you will be in one of the following four categories after reading this book.

1) You will consider the possibilities and may act on them; your mind is open.

2) You will be in acceptance of these discoveries and excited by the possibility of finally having discovered a truth that will return to you immense personal and tangible value.

3) Regretting not becoming aware of what is keeping you from discovering what you do not know you do not know.

Personal regret I can handle with one simple phrase that was given to me by a trusted friend named Kelly some years ago. "Some people never wake up. Just be glad you did."

Part of the idea of creating the box called: 'Something for Nothing' came from that statement, as I struggled to grasp the value in this concept. As regret continued in its attempts at taking me back to the past, something others continued to state as unchangeable, I reflected on his prior words of wisdom. I went on the internet and found a company that would produce a Box for me to experiments with.

4) You will be exactly where you were prior to reading it. You will be stuck on the position of being right. By that I mean that miracles will still be fairy tales often spoken by others as realities. The stress, fear, meanings, worry, boredom, doubt, rejection, fatigue, guilt, fault, regret, not enough time and more will still govern your life as lost time will continue to dine on you, getting fatter on the untapped potential contained within your powerful creative voice.

"There is nothing in a caterpillar that tells you it's going to be a butterfly." © R. Buckminster Fuller

Chapter Eight

Walking the Walk

After I had spent a few hours recalling unique memories from my previous encounter with these two entities and their deliberations, I crawled into bed; laying my head on my pillow for some much needed escape and rest. Within the first five minutes I noticed my lower jaw beginning to twitch uncontrollably. Light concern entered my mind. Then the twitching began to get worse. Fearful thoughts instantly invaded my mind, leap-frogging over my recent gains in knowledge, increasing in abundance as they caused a flush of fear to again grab the totality of my attention. It somehow knew it was time to fish or cut bait.

Just then inklings of knowledge I had gleaned from the R.I. (Recovery International, Dr. Abraham Low, M.D.) training classes I was attending and memories of data I had received during the est (Erhard Seminars Training) rushed back in to alter my perception. At first I asked the twitching to stop, with no results. Then I begged, pleaded and I prayed, yet no results manifested. Then as the twitching continued to invade my reality, I mentally took hold of Dr. Low's teachings and the lessons learned from the est training. Softly, with a twinge of intention, I stepped out of that subjugated box I refer to earlier and spoke out loud telling it to stop. Much to my amazement it stopped. Whew! The thoughts of fear vanished from my mind. Off to sleep, thinking it was just a fluke moment in time. Now the next night, guess what was waiting for me as I lay down to go to sleep? You guessed it, the memory of the night before.

Would it happen again? It did! So, learning from the night before, I firmly told it to stop. It stopped. Again, off to sleep wondering, what just happened? Now come the lessons, the discoveries the cause, and the cure.

I woke up, brushed my teeth and sat down to partake of a cup of tea, reflecting on the events of the last two nights. Instantly a two-inch round stiff steel rod of pain shot down my spine and back area. I felt totally paralyzed for that moment in time and reacted with an inner strength never before experienced. I spoke with the authority of a King proudly sitting on his thrown in absolute alignment with the authority given him. I forcefully spoke out loud to this feeling, illusion, memory and force. I told it to get the { *^#_+~} out of my body, telling it that it was nothing but a trivia. It was gone in that instant. I sat for some length of time in inspired amazement.

This experience was what Dr. Low has asserted in his teachings, saying that a voice is a muscle that becomes stronger when used. This was also very similar to what Werner Erhard, the founder of est had also discovered. Mainly that my voice had an unbelievable amount of untapped power when recognized and appropriated. I then came to realize I had not tapped into its true power to protect myself from things like this. It was then that the memory of what had happened--the cause--surfaced for me to see clearly. The feeling I had experienced when the rush of adrenaline entered my body back in that restaurant was just a feeling of fear that had no power over me until I give it that power. When I laid my head on that pillow the next night I was filled with a grateful peace of knowing that I knew. I had been given a miraculous gift of experiencing something of extreme value, and that in time I would be open to the means of sharing it.

The next day, still basking in the wondrous feelings of gratitude, I mentally reached back attempting to recall what had transpired. I sat on my couch and ever so timidly at first, applied this lesson of 'having power over' certain emotions, thoughts, forces and beliefs in my life. Boredom, worry, guilt, having nothing to do, stress, fatigue, sleeplessness, circumstances, not enough time, too much time, not enough money, lack of, doubt, anger, what will people think, the chatter of my mind, always, never, labeling, judgment, blame, shame, right, wrong, mistake, etc., each surfaced to challenge me. As I spoke aloud to each they turned and ran from me, becoming the illusions they were prior to me giving them power over my life. Over time I did the exact thing with anxiety and slowly the depression and the anxiety lifted. I discovered half of the cause was my perception, my point of view…of thinking I was powerless over the meanings I had allowed society to program me into believing. The remaining chapters are dedicated to the other half of the discovery. The half that completes the whole, the something I was still in search of.

First of all I do understand that fears, meanings, thought, beliefs, events, happenings, dramatic situations, etc., are what you think they are, yet just ask yourself this question. What toll are these reactions taking on your body and your mind? If you just took a moment and practiced thinking and speaking of the situations from a different point of view, what would your body and mind feel? If you just take a moment to think this through, the emotional stress, worry and fear are all a waste of your life force and your energy. I discovered a way to transform them.

Now you know. You have the knowledge and the understanding. You could choose to believe it, yet by reading about my experiences, does it allow you to taste the joy of knowing that you know? Reactions like 'I know that' and 'so what' were clever little responses that were readily thrown around during the est training I attended as I attempting to grasp the asserted value of this gift of discovery. There is a part of our mind that thrives on knowing and so it steals the real value, so as not to loose its control of our lives and our points of view. As Werner Erhard and Dr. Low attempted to transfer their combined experiences that surfaced from what they had both discovered to be true, it was of this hurdle of human's regurgitating 'thinking they already knew' (their past programming}) or understood that they both encountered.

One of Dr. Low's quotes fits this perfectly. "If my patients had more patience I would have fewer patients." When Werner's attempted to pass along what he had learned he also encountered this babble of 'thinking we knew' so he came up with brief annoying phrases like; 'What's so' and 'so what.' As he attempted to impart his wisdom, his insights and his values, these little phrases became part of the responses necessary to meet the challenge of overcoming the mind's automatic response, that of being right.

Being unaware of being on the position of being right, thinking we already know, stops us in our tracks when it comes to discovering who we are and what we are capable of. I know now we do not have a clue as to the power we possess within or the power of our potential! The est training I mention here dealt with something few can even comprehend. It explored: 'What we do not know we do not even know.' It is within this arena that there are real discoveries, yet it takes a commitment to giving up the position of being right and thinking that we ourselves, already know. The costs of hanging onto being right and thinking we know are now permeating this planet as we speak. Divorces, wars, fights for territory, fighting for space, the war on drugs, religious wars, etc., are all based on the arrogance of being right. Too many human beings are at the effect of being right and thinking that they know the truth--the right point of view. All points of view are valid and yet they are just points of view. Sadly, many are not aware of this being a position they are on; therefore they cannot see the cost of defending it.

Being unconsciously stuck on a position can run and ruin your whole life as each of the positions creates distance in relationships, both personal and in business. We think we have to defend ourselves from those we are attempting to relate to. Subtle resentments slowly build up within, causing loss of your true self and over time the relationships. And yes, you are right. This Book and a Box is just my point of view and no, I am not on a position as there is nothing to defend.

Chapter Nine
Thought Control vs. Peeling the Onion

When I first took on the daunting challenge of attempting to gain control over my thoughts, I kept detailed records of the results that appeared. For years it was random, hit and miss with little or no consistency. Even though the numerous attempts at controlling my thoughts manifested into occasional moments of value, I saw that it excluded many people from reaping the benefits promised by attempting to control the plethora of thoughts that permeate their minds at random. To gain control over their thoughts by the very thing that did the thinking became an arduous, somewhat futile task.

These early years of effort and discipline led me to notice that there was something that seemed to be missing among the mass agreement of 'thought' being this creature that had control of our actions and our lives. Over time the premise that 'thought' had to be tamed and brought under control by thinking became like attempting to control a metaphorical Tasmanian devil that had experienced the effects of being addicted to crack cocaine. As this mind attempted to acquire, attain, get, possess, dominate, control and manipulate people and things outside of themselves, the need for the drug of attention and control became its main means of surviving. It ran peoples lives leaving them stripped barren of self worth. I began to notice that the more effort I put in to controlling this powerful, cunning and baffling elusive little devil the more it fought back. Over time I began to discover that it loved control and attention was its favorite meal, causing the addiction of thinking thoughts by thinking increased in its severity. It became like being on a roller coaster loop with no designated exit point in sight.

As I studied the premise of cause and effect for some 40 years, I stumbled upon a question that caused me to look deeper into the possibility that thought also had within it the makings of cause and effect. What causes thought was the question I asked myself. What is the source of its power? Where does it originate and become this power we give it? As we go through life it seems to just show up at random moments, causing havoc on our lives and the lives of others. Mostly these thoughts are like a gnat buzzing around a pile of rotting fruit, nipping at us through out the day. Swatting them causes frustration to boil within us, ignoring them allows them to multiple and thinking about how to rid ourselves of the annoyance only annoys us more. There must be a way of finding peace and I was on a mission to discover that peace.

Many books have been written on the topic of attention being the answer to this dilemma of thought control, yet even these have been lacking in results of returning the person to their true self, the self with original authority over these thoughts that think. I began to notice that even the thought of not giving attention to something is actually giving attention to it, causing more attempts at thought control, ad infinitum.

This, 'What you give your attention to you get more of' comes from other teachers which I have also studied in length only to find it also missing something that to me is now obviously the missing something withheld from the listeners. As I took a moment to step back and listen and observe, I began to notice what was going on during all the question and answer conversations that showed up at seminars, cassette and video tapes and in books. The teachers were causing thought while expounding on the virtue of controlling it, and they are doing this with the one thing we all have in common, their voice, their speaking. The simple story about fish shows up here to illustrate my point. I see it as them feeding people fish, not teaching them how to fish. This book is about showing you where the big fish are hanging out so you can eat them (recognize and appropriate them) for dinner.

Through much effort and self discipline I came to a place where the thought of; 'There must be a faster, easier, more powerful way' began to dominate the very process of that statement and it began to materialize into being something by which I controlled the means to this end. Could this something have within it the something I was in search of? Asserting that there might be faster, easier, more powerful way, and might even include a little fun along the way along the path of discovery might be a little presumptuous on my part and that was okay with me. I know that much time has passed since James Allen put pen to paper and offered his insights to the world for consideration. The world has evolved over time and thought has expanded to include new possible views and premises that were once given to be impossible that are now becoming absolute new truths. The past programming has had its fifteen minutes of fame,, and now is the time for you to take hold of the wheel of the million-dollar yacht (your life) you were given and steer the damn thing.

One of the catalysts of my discoveries came from a seemingly innocent, well known expression that is casually thrown around and spoken from the point of view of 'the truth.' Personally, I have heard many say that there is 'no such thing as something for nothing.' This phrase was and is an unconscious belief that over time has been spoken as 'the truth' and silently morphed into the conversation as though it were blatantly obvious.

It is spoken as though this 'something for nothing' does not exist. It is also spoken as though the value of 'nothing' is an absolute knowing and when heard as 'the truth' it keeps hidden the true value of this thing we call nothing. Without the moment of nothing preceding a note, music would not be.

"Everything would be static. There could be no motion between bodies, no music minus silence, no rhythm without pause, no meaning without space between words and sentences, no emptiness out of which new thoughts, new works, might arise. We find 'nothing' in science. We find it in art. We find it in the philosophies of Hegel, Heidegger, and Sartre.... We find it in the plays of Samuel Beckett. We find it in the poems of Emily Dickinson, Robert Frost, and Rainer Maria Rilke. We couldn't calculate, compose, or create without nothing." © By Joe DiMaggio, MD

So now we have two simple words spoken unconsciously into the psyche of the human mind: 'nothing' has no value and that 'something for nothing' does not even exist. This is a perfect example of making something disappear. If we just turn that statement on its head, or just look at it differently, it might be more like; "All of something of value came from nothing." Kind of like the theory/story/belief of the big bang.

Well, maybe not, was the insight that revealed its presence to me. As literal as the statement of there being 'no such thing as something for nothing' is, it has been spoken with great authority by those who profess a knowing, notably by Napoleon Hill. © "There is no such thing as something for nothing."

Fortunately, my desire to pin point the presence of the something that was missing allowed me to question the validity of that past statement. If you, like I did, tuned your listening to those who have actually experienced this phenomenon called nothing, it is spoken from a different point of view. Many very wealthy individuals have stated this in the past that they started from nothing. Many have also stated that if it was all taken away they could create it again from nothing. What do they know that is kept as a secret from those searching for this secret...this truth?

Might it be that those who have discovered this truth place a different value on this slippery notion of nothing? Do they see it from a different point of view? Do they know something we don't know that has taken us over with the power of others assertiveness, leaving us still searching. What is it that they might know that keeps most of us searching and guessing about this nothing's origin, location or substance? Why is it not explained or shared with the masses? Is it spoken from a consciousness of lack or scarcity? Is it just for the chosen few? And if so, why? Is there a shortage of this something for nothing? If there is a shortage of this thing called something for nothing that would mean it would be a rare thing to find, right? When something is rare isn't it extremely valuable? Is it difficult to acquire, complicated by its very nature? Moreover, if it does not even exist, might it be something that became extinct? No longer in existence, lost or especially having died out leaving no living representatives.

I now know that it is not complicated, not only for the chosen few, not in short supply, not extinct, not difficult to acquire and yet it is spoken from the consciousness of lack and or scarcity. It is the language of 'nothing' which is of true value. Everything, including the world we reside in came from nothing. All progress comes from nothing and this nothing is within us all. We have been conned into believing that we have to get something and that something is more valuable than the nothing we already have.

If an auction were held offering something or nothing, what would we pay the most for? We value something over nothing. We have become getters not receivers, takers not givers, while the past beliefs in regards to shortage and lack run amuck causing us to act as if it is real. Working hard, keeping your nose to the grindstone has become the norm, being verdurous in it's very nature. We have something to strive for, while those who profess gaining understanding withhold the value of experiences, while reaping the benefits of this knowing of a simple secret once available to the masses.

I have watched and listened over the many years of my life and continue to discover the many cons placated on 'we the people' all in the name that it is for the good for the whole; that we do not know this secret. It is the 'collective unconscious' or 'they'; both terms being interchangeable from this point forward, that state these seemingly truths--mostly untruths that squelch the very essence of who we are as human beings. Like mice lost in the maze of confusion we continue to search for the external cheese of value seldom recognizing what is within.

If you picture a new swimming pool filled with clear water representing who we are at birth, and then add one tiny drop of black ink for every manipulating point of view placed in our minds by those who speak of knowing, you will have a black pool of confusion. How many clear water drops would it take to get back to clear water of nothing? Such is the challenge.

This force, this overbearing stream of notions, beliefs, do's and don't, say this, say that, think this, think that, etc. are slowly sucking the life blood out of humanity while band aids are being placed on the sores of those being most effected. Very few are dealing with the causes as those effected are mounting in numbers as they attempt to cope. Something is amiss, foul in nature and rotting at its core. What could this invisible force be? Can it be stopped or has it tipped the scale toward hopelessness? Could there be a power like Superman coming to save the day? Some say no. I say it is possible.

What I am suggesting is not new in discovery, yet it is new in scope. Sometimes humans have to be pushed to the brink of first-hand experiencing terrible consequences before they act. Living a life of doubts, quiet desperation, fears, struggles, addictions and diseases has become acceptable and now somewhat commonplace, not to be questioned anymore as to the cause of any of them.

Negative events are reported as nauseam, rumors of doom and gloom, newly discovered diseases and powerless over this and that. Stories of people being victimized continue to multiple, being regurgitated over and over until finally becoming illusions of realities, burying any real truths, squelching opportunities from surfacing in the face of having to confront disagreement. Taking the position of being right overweighs logic and turns into hatred arguments and sometimes the death of those who are stuck in the plights of right and wrong discussions. Not necessarily the permanence of real death, but the agonizingly slow tedious death of a soul who has lost touch with who they are underneath the need to think and feel that they are indeed 'right'. Not being aware of the fact of being out of touch with their true nature and thinking it is okay.

It is like a war of divide and conquer as this invisible force continues to undermine the once known obviousness of common sense. People walk around like zombies, marching to the rhythm and shuffle of being lost, searching for solutions or insights in all the wrong places. At the time of this writing, television and the internet offers as entertainment; "The Walking Dead." Their statistical studies reveal to them that this is what we want to view. The saddest part is that we believe this hogwash. We continue to allow our subconscious mind to be programmed, refusing to think and speak for ourselves from the position of power. The choice to think for ourselves is just to damn hard as it may upset the very people we love. OMG! When did we begin the slide down the slope into the quick sand of oblivion? Is there a bottom?

Another simple statement, yet a statement that has gained power over mankind is, 'History always repeats itself.' It lands directly in the psyche of mankind, causing a powerlessness to settle within while the obvious reality of constant change is continuing to be buried in wet cement of non-think. You might rebel against what I see; that of 'we the people' being at the effect of what 'they' say is real, yet the evidence is staggeringly obvious once the veil of naivety is stripped away. Every moment in time we are given the opportunity to transform ourselves, therefore history, yet the statement itself blocks seeing and celebrating the gains we make. We the people continue to regurgitate past issues and meanings, recreating them ad nauseam as we are stuck in being right about this ridiculous joke of; 'If Pete and Repeat were sitting on the fence and Pete fell off, who would be left?...Repeat," being an accepted way to improve our lives.

We are left with enormous struggle and effort as being the only way to change, spending copious amounts of money in the attempt in finding our lost selves. We are thinking, believing and acting like broken beings trying to fix a brokenness that is simply the choice of allowing conversations of powerlessness and helplessness to permeate our psyches. We try as we may to block this force with thoughts of refusing to let it in, yet within that refusal, the resistance, lies the very problem:

"Whatever you resist, persists." © Carl Jung. © Albert Einstein said that, "Energy never get destroyed, it can only change form."

In times past subliminal messages were hidden in some musical vinyl records and/or recordings that were broadcast to the public all in the attempt at programming us into believing something of which we were not aware. Now as time has progressed and thinking for one's self has become unfashionable amongst the newest generation, the messages are now blatantly and unashamedly spewed across the medias of your choice. It is no longer necessary to attempt to hide the messages from being heard or seen as there are few with enough intellect to think for themselves, let alone any thoughts of the long term effect it may have. Live for the now is the new motto spoken and lived, the hell with the future as fewer believe there will be any future. There is a saying I heard once that states an interesting premise: The way to program and control a society is to eliminate just one generation's beliefs and standards. Watch your TV...they are close to that goal. Do you see it?

"If history repeats itself, and the unexpected always happens, how incapable must Man be of learning from experience.?" © George Bernard Shaw

Chapter Ten

The Weight of a Thought

As I took on the challenge of exposing the flippant mysterious veil of this something, it seemed to me that this something was indeed present and at the same time, discoverable. I began to study thought energy. Energy is everywhere and in everything. I focused on the possibility of this something coming from the big bang theory. Was it present prior to the something that is now in the present? Was this something not, and then it was. Where was this something before the universe and human beings arriving if it was everywhere and in everything?

Thought within itself is energy, as it is something, so I agree and recognize Mr. Allen's premise as to the value of thought having power, but still there is this something, this something that is missing. Where is this something located if not being contained within thought? If it is everywhere and it is in everything, then everyone must already possess this energy. Who knows of the existence of this something that is missing? Is it within those who know of this energy, within those who know the secret, within those who can harness its power? When did this energy become available? Possible answers: It was available at the moment of the earth's becoming. We were born into this energy, and now it surrounds us, as it is everywhere and it is in everything. It is nothing and we are surrounded by it.

If, as I have asserted, all is energy, I mean everything on the planet and beyond. I include that even thoughts are energy. Scientists have inquired into this mystery for many years and they all come up with the same conclusion: that even inside an atom's nucleus there is nothing able to be observed except energy—and that very energy changes merely by the act of observing. They can't measure it, can't see it, can't touch it, but something, somehow illusive is there, and it changes with every observation. It can be used and placed inside something, the atom bomb proved that. The results or effect of staking my claim on discovering this something that was missing started to generate tiny bits of wisdom, hints as to the possible of it existence.

This something that was missing was located somewhere and everywhere--and it is pure energy. As I continued to study energy, I encountered an abundance of questions. What is the weigh of a thought? What is the weight of a word? Does each letter have weight within a word? If a thought is thought quickly, does it have the same weight as a thought being thought at a slower speed? Who cares? How about the silver-tongued knowers that attempt to con us into believing that more is less? How could I prove that these questions even have answers?

I experimented with thinking a thought, attempting to feel its weight. Then I spoke the thought, attempting to decipher a difference. Which has the most energy, which has more power, which gives you more control, thought or speech? Weight then took on a different meaning, a different essence, once I thought it through and experienced it first hand. I ran through a repertoire of words, first just thinking them. Hate = heavy, rock = heavy, confined = heavy, lack = heavy, debt = heavy, disease = heavy, worry = heavy. Then song = light, feather = light, freedom = light, pebble = light, abundance = light, spirit = light, health = light. Then I spoke these same words out loud to myself and I could feel the subtle distinctions of weight. I have not scientifically weighed a thought or a spoken word, but based on this experience, I am asserting that speech has more energy, weight and power than thought.

It then became obvious to me that I had been mislead into believing I had a minimum amount of power or control, and the meaning to life was not knowable. The proof: I had not succeeded in gaining control of my thoughts. It was then that I caught a faint, somewhat illusive glimpse of this something I had been searching for as it instantly appeared in the moment only to slowly fade from my grasp.

Wisdom it seems, comes into each of our lives at certain times and for a certain purpose. It is as though it knows what we need to do, to be, to evolve. What steps we need to take that would allow us to see what is stopping us from reaching the true discovery we are seeking.

For many years of my life I have been blessed to have such a source of wisdom close enough that I can go for a visit when I need a bit of this wisdom. She is always able to see what I can't see when I am to close to it. It is as though she is able to create a calm clearing that magically appears where once there was confusion. Her wisdom: "Let it go, as it does not matter." As I let it go, where there was something, was now nothing.

My next insight was to let go of what I had accepted as 'the' truth. Searching for 'the' truth became another fallacy. Simply spoken, I was about to discover the obvious, that there are many, many truths. What else to let go of was the next of many lessons. Learning how to was not an easy task.

Many years passed as I gained more and more understanding in regard to this thing called letting go. Two or three questions replaced every answer as I traveled on this highway of letting go. Izy, my muse came into my life in the late 90's as a gift, a reward for my efforts regarding writing. He showed up late one night as a tiny yellow light bulb doing a dance upon the keys of my Mac to assist me as I was writing a book about ideas. He sparked this letting go, while encouraging me to discover my own audacity. Muses are, as far as I know, not an every day event that happens to a lot of people. Why me was just one of the questions that permeated my waking hours when he came for a visit, so I asked him; "Why are you coming to me to write these silly books about ideas that, once spoken create aliveness?" His response was simple, straightforward and to the point. "Trust me, I know what I know." So, I let go again into evermore. The next Chapter is a brief excerpt from that book.

Chapter Eleven

Victims of the Voice

It was noon, December 26th on my 60th birthday that my muse "Izy" first came to visit me. He came at a very troubling part of my life. Financial setbacks had left me, to say the least, down and out for the count. I found myself back at my parent's home, out of a job and my Chevy van was on its last leg. It was when a good friend came by to visit and confronted me about the rut I had somehow gotten myself into that this idea started to stir into becoming.

"Whatever you want to do on your birthday, just do it," she said, as if it was no big thing. As my mind raced forward to my lack of funds, I remember mocking her seemingly impossible statement because my wish was to write a book. A book about what I had learned from my direct experiences in life. Most of what I had learned was in direct opposition to what I had been told to be true. This left me with a bone to pick with someone, but that someone was not to be found. I felt conned and was beginning to see that others had also been conned. This insight had been born from a place of observance, watching and listening for answers to questions no one seemed to be looking for. Is this it; is this what life is all about? This was the predominate question that I seemed to find no answer to.

For over 25 years I had repeatedly told anyone who had a birthday that they could do anything they wanted to do on their birthday. I had observed over time that there was a whole lot of agreement out there for it being a magical day. I always wondered why this was so and then one day I saw why it was so. A light went off in my head. There was power in agreement. Little did I know by speaking those words about birthdays, about what I had observed, that they would come back to bless me in the future.

I felt the pressure subside once my friend left, yet the more I thought about her words, the more I tried to push them aside, the more a part of me chewed on them. I was continually entertaining the idea of writing a book ... why not? I mean, what else did I have to do? It would not cost me anything but time and I had plenty of that. The question and statement hung in the air going back and forth—gotcha!

So I let myself get caught up in the question. I looked around my room and found a notebook and a pen. Then I wondered about where to go to get in the writing mood. There was a lake nearby, why not there? I asked myself, but no excuse came.

I drove over to the lake and found just the right place to park. I found a tree that shaded my van, overlooking the calming beauty of the water. I watched the ducks and geese float around the lake, seemingly without a care in the world and I was at peace with all that was. Just then envy raised its ugly head. Envying ducks and geese, man ... this is really sad. Somehow I slipped into the space of creativity, picked up the pen and flipped open the notebook exposing the blank pages within.

The first question to come to mind was a title, what was the title of my book? That's when my muse showed up. What popped into my head was an Idea. Now, I have had ideas before, yet this one was very different as it had a profound power of focus. It came as a picture of a little light bulb with a voice that told me his name was "Izy." I ignored it, thinking humm, maybe I ought to take a nap. I heard myself snap at him and told him I was searching for a title, not an Idea.

Strangely enough he took it in stride and said in a clear voice, abruptly sure of himself. "Don't worry about the title Vic. I have a birthday gift for you. If you will listen and write down what I have to say, I will grant you your birthday wish."

At that moment I slipped into another realm of consciousness. I spent the next five hours playing with the thoughts and questions that came flooding into my mind. I was taking a Landmark Forum seminar that was about asking the right questions and listening for the answers and this experience mirrored the time I spent at the lake.

Now I have heard many thoughts and questions rattling around in my head, who hasn't, but this was very different. I was experiencing these thoughts take me over, leading me into the unknown. I had dropped my inhibitions before, this was somewhat similar, and so I mentally went along for the ride. Looking back I see now I was experiencing the present. Not as a word, but as an experience. Some part of me was willing to stay in that present moment and then the next moment after that. I was listening and writing. An athlete would call it "being in the zone."

The hours flashed by and I wrote as fast as I could, imploring Izy to slow down, as I kept getting caught up in questioning the sanity of it all. His excitement overwhelmed me, yet I didn't question the direction or the outcome. I never thought about the time or questioned the purpose of any of it. Then at the end of the five hours he said with the calmness of a preacher, "We will meet again when you are ready," and poof ... he was gone.

I slowly came back to reality and headed home. I grabbed a bite to eat and went to my room, saying nothing to anyone about what had just transpired. Much to my surprise Izy was in my room waiting.

He said, "It is still your birthday. Fire up your computer and let's get this writing down in some form you can see and hold in your hand as a book to be published someday. You have to learn from some experiences in your future, but we will need this as a solid format."

Was this weird, spooky, strange, unreal? Yes, it was, and you haven't heard the best of it. I fired up my Mac, which made me smile as I watched the happy face appear as it hummed into action.

It was late at night and the lighting from the neon light above my Mac created a mood that was just this side of spooky. "Okay, I can do this. I have the time and it might even be fun," I said to myself, thinking no one was listening.

As I opened up a blank page on my Mac, the words "Victims of the Voice" came out of nowhere. It was the book title I had asked for. My mind went immediately into questioning the Idea, "Where did that come from?" I asked myself.

Izy was extremely persistent and said, "Never mind, let's go! Time is a wasting."

Twice in one day I stepped into this other 'dimension.' This was not the 'I' as I had known myself to be. I was beginning to experience writing as fun instead of work, like an "E" ticket ride at Disneyland. "Okay, let's get going," I relented. "I will type these words and put them in a recognizable form for the future."

As I began to type the strangeness of this adventure took on a completely different form. I started to visualize little half-inch 'Ideas' looking like light bulbs hovering around my keyboard and all of them were begging to get into the story. Each one would start to bounce around on the keyboard trying to get my attention. Catching my eye, they would begin to glow just bright enough to let me know that they were there. One ran back and forth along the 'F' keys of my keyboard while another Idea jumped over him. Still another did a summersault off the 'ESC' key, and then upon his landing he did the splits. Other little Ideas were doing spins on the number keys and one even did a jig. This was a pure unadulterated delight for me. I typed for three hours straight, spell checked, edited and revised until my eyes could focus no more. I was sorely in need of a break. Little did I know when I took it that it would last for the next ten years!

"Ninety-nine percent of who you are is invisible and untouchable." © R. Buckminster Fuller

Chapter Twelve

Is this Something Real?

I then began to ask questions while letting go of the need for answers and much to my surprise this practice opened up my mind to the freshness of new ideas. I was able to grasp the freshness of change being what is. We all fight change, needing to have some sense of control, yet when enlightenment raises its powerful presence, we all have a choice. Either we fight the battle of futility by hanging on to what doesn't produce the results we desire or we go along for the ride of letting go of the past programming. I too have purposely embraced this thing called change, attempting to let go of the past. Each time I would notice the amount of effort and repetition required.

What I discovered as I continued to practiced the premise of letting go was that I was still mentally giving attention to the past. I then began to wonder if there might be an easier, faster way to get the results I desired. A distant question surfaced, replacing the wondering. What is missing? I remembered this quandary from the est training I had done in the early 70's. Stated as a fact: 'what is missing' is discoverable and it is located somewhere. The following inquiries are about what I discovered while searching and finding 'what is missing' along with the discovery of the location of that somewhere.

I have not by any means become a master of the use of this something, but I have glimpsed some of its illusive yet fascinating rewards. I cover the discoveries of the easier, faster, more powerful way, that of transforming the past throughout the following chapters and in How to use the Box

Please wait until you finish this book until you read (How to use the Box.)

As I continued this inquiry into discovering what was missing, I began to observe people--listening deliberately and intently, hearing mostly the universal struggle and disillusionment of many. I began to notice the byproducts produced by this accepted truth of thought--control being the way to gain mastery over one's life. What showed up in many encounters were dissatisfaction and frustration. The premise of acquiring control over my thoughts in order to gain power over them, and the act of relentlessly looking for the meaning of life was presenting itself to me as futile. I knew these mysteries had been pondered long before we had discovered the miracle of flight, the internet and many new theories regarding how the mind and the universe works and I found myself stuck within known ways of thinking and beliefs regarding finding any answers with the merit I was searching for. I was soon to discover and experience something else about this box of controlling thoughts we all seem to be subjugated to live in.

One day as I was focused on finding this missing something, I overheard two people speaking to each other about some things they had discovered about life. The conversation starred out at the level of the newness and the freshness of discovery, yet as each person attempted to pass this information over by speaking to another, there was this something that thwarted the exchange of information and the joy of sharing an experience. This something was invisible, yet it seemed to have the power to interrupt the flow or exchange of something of great value.

It is of this something that I want to address. If, as suggested in Mr. Allen's book, thinking is what is given the power and value, why does this way of thinking and speaking stop real value from entering our lives? Maybe this type of thing called thinking is actually a hindrance, something that robs each of us the value of something we crave; yet do not know how to get it. Maybe it is something we do not even know is missing. Maybe this thinking itself is in control of something in us, robbing us of something we want for ourselves. Might it be something like support, value, attention, acknowledgement or recognition? Maybe the feeling of being present? The excitement of being alive? Might it be something that is robbing us of our sense of satisfaction and completeness?

I then noticed something during another conversation. When each person was thinking thoughts, then speaking in the attempt of conveying an idea or discovery to the other, they were attempting to place something in the place of another something with the same weight and power as the first something. To the casual observer, this could be seen as a form of communication or a means of exchanging ideas or thoughts, yet I saw it as using fire to fight fire, the flames of habitual thinking or programming continuing to burn. I began to notice that something was missing in this exchange as it often left people lacking the feeling of satisfaction and it also left him or her with a sense of frustration. Why didn't satisfaction materialize within this exchange? Why didn't the sense of pleasure appear? Something was there that thwarted the exchange, and again this something was missing from my awareness. Was there something missing that could facilitate the sense of satisfaction and remove the frustration?

In the example above, for the most part, there is an expectation of something and the results seem to be dismally low. One of the things I also began to notice missing in this exchange of thoughts and speaking was not only the lack of results, but also the lack of enjoyment, excitement and fun. There was not much power or energy exchanged in this endeavor to control thoughts. It became not only pointless, but very serious business, taking up valuable times in each one's life. I also noticed the return on the investment of time and energy was not fulfilling the expectations of each. It was similar to placing money in the bank and discovering that the fees were eroding the minimal interest rate offered in exchange. My quid pro quo scale began to tip again, raising its awareness, intending to be heard.

Something had to shift, so I asked myself this question: If energy is in everything and it is located everywhere, what was the source of this energy and how and what does it produce?

The illusive glimpse I had received previously--this something mysteriously morphed into an epiphany. A single voice created all that is. Power, control and meaning all come from a thought first...yet does 'thought' have the same power as a voice? I can 'think and feel' panic in an airplane and no problem arises. Once spoken, the power of the thought is released and it causes a reaction. As I began to really look at this epiphany's message, I could see that everything created after the earth's appearance started with a thought, I agreed, yet what was it that transformed the earth into the form of this time/space reality? The spoken word! Words were spoken into the space of nothing and became. "In the beginning there was the word". Now, I know many 'understand' this, yet I will assert something here that might upset your belief cart.

"Understanding and knowing are distinct and understanding is the booby prize." © Werner Erhard.

"The Only Source of Knowledge is Experience." © Albert Einstein.

One of the benefits of having studied the discipline of cause and effect for some years is that it enabled me to stumble upon a few questions that raised their heads demanding recognition. They were similar to the quandary of, "Which came first, the chicken or the egg?" Do these thoughts just appear out of thin air, or is there something more to it? What is the effect of thoughts appearing in this manner if a cause is present? Possible answer: Thought thinks us. Do thoughts stand-alone or is there something that causes the effect they have on us as humans? The effect they have over us is the power we unknowingly and unconsciously gave them.

I say the thoughts that think us are tainted, coming from past programming and are not authentic to our true nature. They are experienced as having power over us. These thoughts from our past lack the power to create as they come from something as apposed to nothing.

I wanted to know the origin, the cause of thought, the source of this energy, this something I was in search of, so I purposely disciplined myself to focus on and stay within these questions. While attempting to observe past thoughts appearing in my own mind, answers were plentiful, yet they lacked the authenticity of absolute recognition.

They were thoughts, of this I was clear, yet they were not thoughts I had consciously chosen. As I experimented with this, questioning itself became very difficult as though the very answers were bombarding me at every twist and turn, thwarting my intention to trace their origins. It was as though the asking of the question created a space within my mind to go into an extreme search mode. As every answer continually presented itself as the authentic one, I eventually saw the ruse and was finally able to discover their lack of originality. These thoughts, these answers were all coming from memories, radio programs, media and television programs, commercials, movies, seminars I had attended, people I have known. Some were religious beliefs, thoughts placed there by my teachers, my parents and they all had one thing in common: they came from the past, and their origination was from somewhere outside of me. The expression of 'incoming thoughts' is a great description. They thought me. I was at the effect of these thoughts. They controlled my thinking; they controlled my life.

Over time I became a disciplined observer of these thoughts, viewing them as they appearing at random. I would close my eyes and there they were, dancing across the screen of my mind, each having a different characteristic, some even appearing with distinct, colorful and unique personalities. As I began to view these thoughts with intense purpose, I began to notice that each thought or word was encased in something similar to an emerging cocoon, creating our given language of understanding. Some of these thoughts or words looked familiar; others were foreign to my knowing. It was the cocoon of encasement that captured my curious nature, so I increased the intensity of focus and my desire to know what these cocoons represented. At first I discovered the obvious: they represented the meanings and feelings that had been placed on them when language was first created. Then it struck me--this was possibly the insight into the something I was in search of. An encasement or cocoon represented a possible becoming, a meaning and a birth into something new, similar to a butterflies becoming. Were these thoughts, past meanings and feelings predestine to become clones of their pasts, or were they awaiting the birth of newness?

I say words arrived first, were recognized and appropriated by man speaking them. Their gift, their freedom of expression, their power was a given available to all, to be used for the purpose of creating freedom or bondage. Over eons this gift of the spoken language had been used to uplift, encourage, support, create feelings, invent, gain power and also diminish, entrap and instill fear within us all. These thoughts, spoken from the language of the past, once having power over me, were refusing to be spoken encased within the cocoons of entrapment or powerlessness. My language also refuses to be born as something or another's power over me. The power of the words I had been speaking had been distilled, distorted, misused, pickled and diluted, placed within the cocoons of the past. The gift of their power would only be returned to the possible future of being spoken into a new becoming.

We do not own our gift, our voices of power. We have become victims of other's voices living rent free inside our minds. The words, thoughts, meanings, beliefs and feelings are presently held up as being ultimate powers, yet we are the ones who were first given the gift of thinking, feeling, and speaking their meanings into existence, therefore aligning with their life force. Something is amiss here.

An example of owning our own power would be the men who wrote the Declaration of Independence. "What they were doing was promising the people of the colonies, that they were giving for them and the Nation; their lives, their fortunes, their sacred honor; Honor was/is sacred because God would judge them based on the integrity, ethics, and moral character that they displayed in life." © Foundation Truths. They were living as being their word given to themselves and to us. Did those words create who they were?

As to the insight I was struck by, it is this. Didn't learned scholars place the meanings that are attached to words some thousands of years ago? Weren't those words recognized and appropriated by the signers on the day of our Declaration of Independence being created? I say they recognized, appropriated language and created a concept called the Declaration of

Independence. They created something from nothing, something that wasn't into something that now is. Concept created a context that containing contents.

Have we been conned or drifted away from owning the power of those words that caused feelings of; 'We the People' spoken some many years ago, thinking they are now just words without the power they once possessed? Have those words and ideals been subtly incased in cocoons of someday becoming alive again and is their plight predetermined to repeat itself? By whom? Might we have been taught that certain meanings are obsolete? Are we capable of separating the past meaning from a word, then attached a new meaning to it ourselves? Could we even think the thought; "words have meanings subject to our choice," let alone change or dismiss a feeling that is attached to it? Are these once spoken words now based on the past scholars having limited knowledge of now? Could we be told that more is less and act on this? Could killing be altered to mean disposing of? Could independent thinking become extinct? Could war be seen as 'trying' to win? Could the power of the words spoken to us and about us somehow cause us to accept the feelings of being powerless? I say it can and it is being done as I write, evident by the presence of political correctness gone amuck. Addressing humans as unable to handle the truth, as we are powerless and weak minded. Dumbed down, desensitized and spoon feed baby food while those in power continue to usurp more power over the masses.

The words, 'As a Man Thinketh', contain nothing but letters strung together creating words. No power, no control, no meaning of life other than common letters or words. They came, I presume, from the thoughts of Allen and were offered from the desire to make a positive difference to those who would read his works. Just as the letters and words, 'As a Man Speaks', so it is', come from letters and words strung together in my mind, becoming thoughts I speak, originating from the desire to make some positive difference.

I then began to notice the possible reason thinking had minimum power or control over my life and did not reveal any meaning to the mysteries of life. Not only that, but I was not thinking the thoughts. They were thinking me, therefore creating me. These thoughts came from my past with meanings firmly attached to them, robing me of my choices. The issue again became one of training my mind to believe in this something that was missing. Believing in something that, as of now, could not be seen. Something other than this mind that did my thinking that consumed my attention and rebelled against being controlled. There was something there, as I occasional got a sense of it, it had a feeling of strength, an essence. It was similar to a glimpse of a passing moment as it whispers its presence, yet it seemed to continue to taunt me, slipping in and slipping out of my grasp as I attempted to discover its origin. The more I attempted to discover what it was the more its illusiveness continued to display itself, flaunting its secretive nature.

I have spent many years questioning life, playing with opposing principles and theories, looking and listening for that something that might make a huge difference in people's lives and in my own. Searching for this illusive something that contained a spark of truth, promising to give me control, power and meaning to my life, took me on a ride most would not have chosen to take. Many blind alleys appeared, as did failures and disappointments. Broken dreams, thoughts of quitting, loss of personal esteem, guilt, shame, blame, anger, fear, depression and even momentary thoughts of suicide blocked every attempt at removing the wall hiding the spiritual marrow of my discovery.

Then, during a moment of clarity, I got another alluring glimpse of this illusive hidden elixir. I felt its presence. I experienced the possibility of a truth being revealed to me. In that moment in time I thought, maybe, just maybe I could look at this walls of this subjugated box I was trapped in differently. I spoke out loud, "This is a veil, not a wall" and poof, it transformed. The 'wall' 'thought by me' to be a wall, was now only a veil, easily seen through as the illusion it was. It was then that I knew, beyond any doubt that this something was real and it was within reach of those who recognized it as a possibility.

Chapter Thirteen

What is this Something?

It was then that the real fun and challenge began. Knowing that there is this something available, knowing it is real and attainable shifted me into another realm of questioning. I experienced a paradigm shift from 'was there a something' to 'what is this something'? Where is it located? Who knows of its existence? When did it become available? How is it acquired? This began a new treasure hunt as I increased my focus, intending to discover and harness this something.

From the moment of our birth we are instructed, taught how to think, what to believe and how to act. These instructions come mostly from our parents and our teachers at school, not to mention the pressure of our peers. We pay close attention, trusting that this practice will give us the illusive reward—but indeed this something is actually ignored and morphs into becoming the something that is missing.

Man is a sentient being and feeling and thinking a certain way has some benefit with regard to getting along in society, yet what if there was something unseen and unspoken, like a secret known only to those few that controlled the masses. What if this something produced faster results was much easier and the byproduct produced was mostly wealth, health, happiness, peace of mind and fun over the long run? Some might 'think' that if there were an easier way, a faster more powerful way, it would have been discovered long ago. Well, this is the point I want to make clear enough for you to inquire for yourself.

I assert that there is a possible truth that we have been lead to believe is inaccessible. It is located in a brief pause wherein one allows oneself the privilege of stopping for a moment in time to ask yourself a simple question: Could there possible be something I do not know that I do not know? In that moment, the something that appears is the opposite of what I assert IS the something I was searching for. This assessment is based on having staked a mental claim based on directly mining and experiencing the asserted claim of thought being all powerful and personally not finding the power and control over my life or the allusive meaning of life I searched for.

When I chose to hunt for this treasure, I was seeking the same satisfaction that mining and finding gold might deliver to me. I wanted to know where the gold was hidden and feel its presence. The following should be considered simply as a possibility. We are stuck in an act, a truly believable story about whom we think we are. This act is backed up by copious evidence that has been gleaned from the many years of trial and error encounters with life and people and it is mostly based on what we have been taught to think.

If our lives are not running smoothly, we call a friend and complain about life not being fair, blame others for our shortcomings, while continuing to stand firmly on being right about what happened. We hope upon hope that something will change by expressing these words of being powerlessness over something outside of the concept of who we think are. Then there are others that perceive and report to us about the many positive aspects of who they think we are, but our perception of ourselves is much stronger as it is backed up by the evidence of our past beliefs. We mostly reject this input as we think what we were taught to think, we believe what we were taught to believe and we act the way we were taught to act. Or, we do the exact opposite, stick up a few more affirmative sticky notes which is still us being controlled by who we were programmed to become by doing or thinking the opposite.

Now this within itself is not bad, yet the thinking, the believing and the acting are running our lives. If, for an instant you disagree, simply stop thinking, believing and acting like you do now.

This is why affirmations seldom work to alter who we would like to become. Acceptance of this fact is crucial to gaining ground on transforming ourselves back into that which we truly are. After acceptance is seen for what it is you will have the tools to create a true shift in your identity. The label given to this change is held as an 'identity crisis' and it is of this word 'crisis' that a later chapter is dedicated to.

I have previously mentioned the obviousness of one of our established truths; that words have meanings. What I also lightly mentioned was discovering that those meanings, beliefs and feelings were attached to me in my past without my conscious choice. Part of that discovery brings me to this observation.

There is some 'thing', a voice, that is generating, creating and altering those meanings for its own benefit, therefore causing us to feel powerless and you are soon to be presented with an opportunity to recognizing your own voice and if willing, appropriate that voice. When both are done you will be in the space of true choice. Take a moment to look up the meaning of the word 'appropriate'.

"The act of setting apart or taking for one's own use." © Dan Word.

As of now this is what I see. This thing, this voice, is a habit or train of thought that is giving our attention and meaning to the existence of what we call reality. We mostly follow along and conform, while others rebel by giving it no attention or ignore it. We sometimes push against it, reject it, argue with or fight against it. Some try to over power it, con it or trick it, try dodging, denying, overriding or disagreeing with what we see, hear or believe is reality. We are attempting to obliterate reality with this inherited mindset of habitually interacting with what is or was, trying desperately to change or fix the past or present reality. This mind set of perceiving and interacting with what already is, or what was in the past, actually gives it more power Which then causes us to be at the effect of what we think is real, as it reflects back to us who we think we are; somewhat powerless to change of fix either.

This 'thing', this voice, is a habit or train of thought and it is the mind of past. It is addicted, in love with attention and control. It is running our lives and we are loosing our true power by giving it our attention and or denying it. You might think whoa! I must stop/change/fix what already is or was. We all know, as the collective unconscious say we must face reality and change or fix what is broken. We must change what is in order to be happy, to feel accomplishment, to feel of worth. This train of thought is not good or bad, right or wrong, it is just what we have been taught to do. I do understand, as there have been amazing things accomplished using this habit of thinking. Sadly to say, there is another principle that empowers this mind of the past that is addicted to attention and control. Even if we resist giving attention to what was or is, it loves the attention of not giving 'what is or was' attention and it is the same as giving it attention which keeps it in control. Control of who or what? You and your true choice!

"What you resist persists." © Carl Jung.

The devilish side of me wants to end this book right here and have you figure it out, but I will forgo that urge and soon reveal the most amazing part of the puzzle I discovered.

Chapter Fourteen

Your True Choice

"Life isn't about finding yourself. Life is about creating yourself." © George Bernard Shaw

What if, just what if we chose to alter the meanings of words and feelings that have been and are being programmed into us. It is not what you think. Not to long ago we were a nation, a people with a say in the matter of our own lives. We felt the power of our voices and we felt the creation of the power spoken by our forefather's words. Much has happened over the years since we owned our own words and lived as though those words had power. I say it is not too late to recognize, appropriate and once again create your own words with true meaning--your own personal power and control.

How you might ask? Stop the madness of regurgitating meanings others put on you. Stop repeating supposed facts or giving opinions for what you do not know in order to look good or not look bad or belong to the crowd. By only speaking from direct experience or if for some reason you simply do not know something, say the words; 'I don't know.' These words won't bite you. Later on I will explain why those words are actually the cause of ignorance. This is also not what you think.

Okay, I hear you speaking up against what I state here, but this is that something I discovered we don't even know we don't know. One example is this: The word 'they say' has usurped our true power. If you take the time to listen you will hear it spoken over and over again, being held up as the authority, the owner of the power we gave away. That one word has taken us off the hook of being responsible for the thoughts we think and the words we speak, robbing each and every one of us of the true power of our voice, our choices and our human rights. We slowly, subtly became victims of words and the meanings that are being used to disempower and victimize us. I am not singly speaking politics here. I am addressing our own personal lives. We did this to ourselves. We allowed this to happen.

Another long held cliché that has inserted itself into the asserted obviousness of truth is the meaning of the word 'assume'. Labeled as a negative we all know it is to be avoided at all costs. It is an acronym for: 'to make an (ASS out of U and ME), yet the true definition aligns directly the word faith. Here are a few definitions of these two words:

Assume: To appropriate or usurp, to take for granted, to seize, to take upon oneself, to take for granted, to pretend to have, to take over without justifications, to take up or receive into heaven, to take into partnership, to place oneself in, to pretend to have or be, to take as granted or true, to think or assert that something is true or probably true without knowing that it is true, to take or begin to have power or control.

Faith: complete trust or confidence in someone or something, strong belief or trust in someone or something, firm belief in something for which there is no proof, asserting something that is believed especially with strong conviction, strong or unshakeable belief in something, any set of firmly held principles or beliefs, honesty or sincerity, as of intention in business, complete confidence or trust in a person, strong religious feelings or beliefs, a system of religious beliefs.

Can you see the issue at hand? We have become a nation lead to believe that having faith or assuming will make us both looking like asses. Talk about living a life in order to look good, or resist NOT looking like asses. Whew!

This lack of integrity, using excuses to rationalize our past and present, while breaking our word is becoming accepted as the norm. It continues without the slightest regard as to the long term consequences, that of freely giving away the power of your words. Assuming another will deal with us honestly and with integrity could make us look bad, so we lower our standards and we put up with irresponsible people we won't hold accountable for fear of reprisal, fear of upsetting them or causing some form of retaliation.

What I discovered is a way back, a way back to power over

ourselves and the past mental chatter of the mind that is addicted to the attention and control that dominates us on a daily basis.

**** Walkabout ****

One of the treasures I discovered in this world of language and ideas is that certain words have power that are not well understood. It is this phenomenon that calls me to write; a desire to add something back into the world I have lived in. A thank you for the privilege of being allowed to play in this game called life.

I did not see life as a game until I was thrown into life during my divorce. You see I was, to say the least, a bit naïve, maybe a touch of Peter Pan. Worldly wisdom did not interest me even when it was forced on me in school. I knew then, for me it was a waste of time--learning about dates of wars, etc. I wanted to dream, to create and to venture out into the world of spirit and beyond. I wanted to know and experience the freedom we all crave.

My interactions with language sometimes resemble a leisure walk in the park when suddenly my thoughts appear as entities just as real as the grass I am walking on. My thoughts often morph into characters clamoring to be included within these pages, attempting to experience the joy of recognition, the essence of being alive. At other times words deviously plan their escape, back into the freedom of autonomy. Regrets are not a big part of my life now, as I have come to a place of having experienced enough to know what is important to me and what is better left alone.

I will now present you with a glimpse of the something I discovered as a riddle for you to solve:

What is everywhere, contains the power within to create anything you can imagine and controls everyone's life. What something when used, does not diminish its power, actually increases in power and is infinite? What something gives you enormous value simply by recognition and is acquired by appropriation? *** What is something can you take freely and not go to jail?

The answer is: language. Language that is not copyrighted

is free, in abundance and it is everywhere. It is the source of everything and contains all the power any one person could utilize in a lifetime. When you hear a belief, a truth, an experience, a desire or a possibility spoken by another, you can choose to have that for yourself. The spoken word is everywhere and it is truly free, yet most people don't seem to be able to access the true power of language. Sadly, we 'understand' this simple truth. We don't experience it. It is as though it has been hidden from view, a secret never to be told. There is no lack of language--everything comes from language.

"Language is wine upon the lips." © Virginia Woolf

We were all born with the gift of a voice—even those born without a voice have a way to communicate--and along with this voice comes another gift called choice. Like a kid in a candy store, you can use language to freely choose your own flavor for each moment of time. As I will expound on in the following chapters, it is not so cut and dry in the beginning. It takes time and work to alter your past beliefs. I do mean 'your' past beliefs. They are yours, even if they were put on you, jammed down your throat or slipped by you when you were not conscious enough to sift through them as fast as they were thrown at you.
'Choice' is a simple word, but there are multiple tenses used to distinguish the past, present and even the future.
 * Chose: Past tense. If a person is communicating about the past, there is something solid to stand on which we call 'memory'. I chose to get married.
 * Choice: Present tense. When used in present tense, it is used to select something from the many options available. Examples, ice cream flavors. If I know I like chocolate. My choice is chocolate.
Both of these tenses of the word 'Choice' and 'Chose' are spoken from the solid platform of something called: knowing.
 * Choose: Present tense. I choose this or that. In this example it is possible to choose from nothing, no past, no knowing, yet few know of its true power.
 It is when you use the word 'choose' to create a future that something not often recognized is present. It is distinct, as it has

within it power to move you from chasing or trying to get something to attracting it to you. This is the true power of your word. Once this power is recognized, appropriating the future is like choosing, again from the limitless options available. The one thing that is different is what you stand on. When you 'choose' to create a future there is nothing to stand on. No memory, no knowing, no evidence, unless you create nothing from something. Creating nothing from something is the key. You can stand on it like a memory or a choice from the many options available. How? Create 'nothing' as being a something, your word. You already have the something, the something that creates---your voice. With your voice you can create standing on 'nothing' as being powerful and valuable. You can stand on it like a memory or a choice from the many options available.

Still, we have this concept called 'understanding'. Understood these examples have little power. It is when they are experienced that they reveal their true power.

I hope the next statement I am about to make will cause you to think. This something I searched for is free, the gold—whatever you desire--is free! What? Yes, free. You already have what you have been searching for. Where is it located? What is the CAUSE of thought? The title of chapter One contains the answer. "As a Man Speaks, so it is."

This is where you have the opportunity to choose to recognize your voice and appropriate it. You already have the something that is missing from your life. It is free once you appropriate it.

Did you get it? What was your reaction? Does it make more sense now? All of your power is located within Your Voice!

Once again, we are left with this concept called 'understanding as being the booby prize.'

If you will notice, understanding the previous statements alone did not make you thinner, happier, stronger, wealthier or wiser. Simply understanding the answer will not be enough for you to access this power and gain control over your life. Also, understanding that this alone is not enough for you to experience control and power over you life or find the meaning of life, but it can be the beam that lights the way to experiencing life itself.

Now that we have identified the something that is missing, you will be able to notice where this gift is located and why it is free. You may think you already have it, but in reality you don't.

Step one is to proactively, consciously recognize it. The 'act' of recognizing the fact that the power and control are still 'within' your voice.

Step two is to appropriate your voice. To proactively, consciously take is back!

Again, the following quote will guide you to the value, the results this Book and a Box has the potential of producing. It came from two dear friends of mine as they demonstrated to me the workings of creating, generating and producing miracles in one's life.

"Have you ever noticed that when you choose to look at something differently, the something you are looking at changes?" This is similar to the Heisenberg Principal.

Chapter Fifteen

Another Walkabout

At various moments in my life I would go for a visit with Jackie, my sister-in-law or Kelly, one of my best friends, attempting to again grasp hold of this slippery notion, this illusive something I was in search of. I would speak; each would listen, allowing me to create from nothing. I spoke and again they would listen as I searched. I searched; they listened. I discovered and they watched. I did not know I knew. I heard it. I experience joy. I then knew I knew and we celebrated!

Those experiences of listening, speaking, discovering and celebration were not experiences I was accustomed to during my marriage and eventual divorce. They were experiences by me as miracles, as I was beginning to discover what worked within relationships.

A lot of what transpired was due to what I had been exposed to during my experiences during the est training in 1975. My mind was open and my heart was broken during and after the divorce, so I willingly, yet anxiously appropriated information and drove myself to experience the celebrations. One of the most valuable insights I experienced was that of accepting that I had unknowingly allowed myself to be programmed. I was becoming aware of the costs of allowing myself to be programmed, controlled, labeled and subjugated to live within the box I spoke of earlier and I was being presented with the keys to freedom. Becoming aware of and using those keys, (recognizing) and remembering I possessed them, (took them back or appropriated them) unlocking the programming (choosing to think and speak for myself) and discovering how to alter the programming, (create from nothing) was not without strife, diligence and grit. The catalyst of this search for the something I thought was missing came directly from the broken heart of a divorce. They were the ramifications of not being true to myself. That of thinking who I was being based on the past thoughts, actions, meanings and beliefs of the programming (thoughts, beliefs and meanings) I had allow to permeate my being. This was a true game-changer for me.

I would often go for a visit with Jackie, my sister-in-law, being it during my recovery from the effects of the divorce, dealing with the effects of the anxiety and depression or later on when I would be stuck in some thought pattern that was causing me unwelcomed strife. At first I would ask if she was open to having some company. She knew I needed help, but for me to admit it was too overwhelming, as my concept of needing help was only for the weak. Over the years of my marriage and unbeknownst to me, she had watched me change as I slowly lost my identity. This change was subtle, deadly and I was blind to it. After numerous visits, after I began to benefit from her acceptance of me, I became confident enough to actually admit I needed help so my requests and confessions became more honest. I would just tell her I needed someone to talk to. Those feelings of being welcomed, accepted as having worth and being acknowledged, slowly altered my perceptions of mainly myself and over time my life.

When the occasional visit with Kelly presented itself, the insights were very similar, yet he ignited within me the rare strength of a man who knew who he was. It was his dynamic personality and his playful attitudes that drew me to him, like a moth to a flame. He also gave of his time, taking precious time out of his day to listen and more importantly, actually hearing me. At first this was foreign to me, this being heard, yet over time, as I got accustomed to the flow of speaking and attentive listening, he freely shared with me some of the many insights, experiences and the wisdom that had blessed his life. The experiences I was presented with during our friendship are held deeply within a special and sacred place of my heart, the place where memories go just in case you need to draw upon their joy and their strength.

At times when Kelly, Irish to the core, and I would immerse ourselves in the very moment of life, that miracles would often appear at random and we delighted in these glorious experiences.

One particular memory was when I went to visit him in Oregon. We set off on an adventure one afternoon just to see how much trouble we could get ourselves into. As we drove along the Columbia River he pointed out the beautiful scenery along the way, telling me about the guys who ride wind surf boards down the river, both thinking, maybe we might. I knew better than to say 'maybe someday", as I knew his response would be; "Someday is now." We stopped, watched awhile and then continued on. Just ahead we came to The Bridge of the Gods that allowed us to cross over the river, so we took the turn. After a bit, we spotted an abandoned shack looking like it was about 100 years young. Exploring natures we both possessed, so we had to take a look. Maybe we would find the forgotten bag of golden doubloons long ago forgotten. The luck of the Irish had always seemed to follow us on these adventures and we were both open to an appearance. No gold doubloons were found that day; still we chuckled and smiled as our spirits were still riding on the high of the possibility of a visit. After a few hours of driving we headed back and again stopped to watch the wind surfers jump and fly through the air.

Just then Kelly remembered and spoke. "Along the way back, on the left, there is a amazingly unique waterfall called: Multnomah Falls. We should stop by and visit her." Excitement filled my soul, reminding me of the magical moments we both had experienced when I won an eight day and night trip to the Caribbean Islands and chose to take him with me. Upon arrival it was indeed breathtakingly beautiful. As we approached the falls a powerful rush of water plummeted down the face of the mountain enveloping all that was.

As we both entered into this breathtaking moment, becoming mesmerized, we were both in awe of being in the presents of one of nature's magnificent gifts. After a few minutes I noticed a trail on the right leading to somewhere, I did not know where. That instant of discovery captured me as I ran up the trail to see where it would lead me. It turned sharply to the left as I reached the plateau and I took the left. The path lead me to another gift of the fall's offering, that of actually being under the waterfall.

As I stepped in I experienced being contained within the

clear ice-cold water, enveloped within its power and majesty, surrounded by the mist of the gift of its water and the fury of its power. I then took a drink, instantly a wish appeared, unspoken. "I wish Kelly was here in this moment." Within the second came his reply. "I am here." Spooky, I agree, yet the Irish luck had smiled upon us once more and we both smiled with recognition and said our hellos. Just then, much to our amazement, yet right on cue, two beautiful white doves came swooping down to join our moment, flying through the waterfall, then instantly disappearing out the other side. Kelly turned to me and said: "Seems the luck of the Irish is still alive and well." We both exploded in laughter, smiled and I again experienced his humor, as his magical, graceful nature touching my soul.

Chapter Sixteen

The Moment of Now

This is it, that is all there is.

How could *understanding* possibly be the booby prize? Let me go a little deeper into the meaning behind this statement. As an example, from what I have observed by listening and interacting with people, came this discovery. There is no tomorrow. The time is only now. Understanding is like intending to celebrate with that special someone by making reservations in the finest restaurant. You get all dressed up in your finest attire and upon arriving, you order, talk on the phone while eating the paper menu (the memory of eating). What you miss is the experience of drinking the fine wine, enjoying the dinner and most of all you miss the value of being in the company of that special someone.

There is a better way. The white night you wished for is sitting across the table from you right now--as is the princess you rescued from the castle or the prince who road up on his horse. I say understanding is the booby prize because we waste the moments we are given with gossip, complaining, being right about some trivial issue, arguing, blaming, talking about what 'they say', wishing we were somewhere else or with someone else. We spend these precious moments attempting to look good, sound good, acting like we have our {#%^*((#} together, etc. Rather than learning to experience the miracles of the moments we are in, we think what we are taught to think, do what we were told to do and act like we are taught to act. Those miracles are there and they appear once one's point of view has shifted.

I too had heard this supposed bit of wisdom of 'understanding being the booby prize' repeated often and I too thought I understood what was asserted. I then realized I was also caught up in the desperate search of understanding something that was stated to be the booby prize. So, if you had a choice, which you do, which would you choose? I choose to place understanding in a secondary position of value and continue my search.

I asked myself again and again, what could be more valuable than understanding? Just then I remembered something else Werner Erhard had said in one of his classes:

"Nothing is missing. You already have what is missing."

That was the very essence of the training. The concept that I already possessed the one thing that everything came from and will come from in my future rocked my psyche. In that moment, the course of my future was altered.

You already have what you are looking for. It is hidden in plain sight! Like a fish to water, you are blind to it.

Werner Erhard, the founder of est asserted that the something that was missing was language that is created, not language itself. Let me explain this statement. Language that is spoken from a past knowing is just that, language. This language has the distinct value and capability of knowing what it knows from the past. It also has the distinct value of causing understanding to appear from the written or spoken word, therefore learning or knowledge.

Language that is created from within, not standing on the past, spoken from nothing, has real value and power. It is itself a creative act.

What if you took a look at another slice of that proverbial onion and peeled away another layer? As you peel it away, just know upfront that this layer might have a few tears contained within this looking.

Most people would resist the following statement, yet when studied it is in fact a truth nevertheless. "We are all being used by this something and it is language." This is not bad, nor is it wrong, it just is. We are wired (programmed) to accept or resist supposed facts, treating those 'facts' as the enemy instead of using the power of language to create the perception of ourselves and the quality of our lives. We are bombarded by the illusions of the language of others having the power to define us at every stage of our lives and so we learn the lessons intentionally taught by those doing the bombarding. Maybe, just maybe there is more to this something that is missing.

In order to survive we must build walls, shields to stop the advances of certain types and styles of language. Language has become something we must constantly screen, being on guard or defending against certain forms of language, which might upset the apple cart of our reality. Can you guess where this all takes place? Our thoughts. You know, that mind who is in love with attention and control, this mind that causes us to work overtime just to find those illusive moments of peace and quiet. The mind that knows it owns the power and controls your life. Could this mind be robbing us of the moments when miracles appear to be experienced?

Constant sales calls, computer driven calls using the tricks of the trade, you need this, you need that, you won this, send the money here, all it takes is a small amount of money to get your millions that some long lost unknown relative or the King of Nigeria left you. Cons running amuck in the sea of plenty. More is less, don't discriminate, be politically correct, don't talk about religion or politics, don't hurt peoples feeling, global warming is and it isn't, we are innocent until proven guilty, diets work, eggs are good for you, eggs are bad for you, whole milk is bad, skim milk is good, whole milk is good, skim milk is bad, guilt is bad, greed is bad, greed is good, aliens are, aliens aren't, weapons of mass destructions are and now they are not. Aren't these all nauseatingly boring supposed facts used to clutter our minds with useless baubles?

Now if you look at this bombarding from the perspective of cause and effect and as a long term proactive, deliberate, conscious plan to cause people to have to build walls in order to not get conned, it is this. We are totally at the effect. We react or resist reacting, which is still reacting. You can only lead; con or control programed confused people who will not think for themselves. This bombardment causes confusion and mistrust. Over time it creates people who now will not listen to those who are attempting to add value to their life. Everything they hear is basically perceived as a con. It has become a divide and conquer ploy.

We have been lulled to sleep, trapped in the regurgitated powerless conversations. We have ssadly stopped thinking for ourselves, forgetting the joy of experiencing life to the fullest. A blatant lack of responsibility for the language we speak to others comes from this very training. Then, using the excuse that we are being forced to mislead people in order to sound informed and look good, we ourselves become the misguided fools we have been trained to be. We don't hold are ourselves accountable for speaking truths backed by direct knowledge of experiences. We grab onto rumors, sound bites, partial truths, statistics with agendas attached to them, claims, illusionary tales, lies, hope, words with no actions, points of views, meanings, being right, blame and more of what 'they' say is the truth. Again, this programmed way of thinking results in confusion and mistrust amongst the very people we are attempting to connect with, as we must feed the mind of the past that is addicted to and in love with getting attention and looking good.

As of this writing there was a recent news bulletin in reference to a large utility company that included the word unlimited in their sales pitch and they got caught limiting the service. Several media commentators discussed this issue and left the audience with this statement: Now, it is up to us to understand that the word unlimited doesn't mean unlimited.

This is a slippery slope of flagrant unaccountability. They got caught with their hand in the proverbial cookie jar and refused to acknowledge it and accept responsibility for it. This is now an intricate part of the experiences we hear about in regard to those who break the law. Paying a huge fine, yet admitting no fault, accountability or responsibility. Maybe someday we will witness someone in court claiming it as being unconstitutional to hold them responsible for their actions as this precedent is used by their lawyer as supportive evidence.

Chapter Seventeen

Remember the Elephant, Small Bites.

If you take a moment to look at what uses you moment by moment, you will find that it is language. Be it truth or prefabrication, the mind either accepts or rejects what it is being told. This gift of language can be used to benefit or destroy us and eons of time have proven this. Once we become aware of the something that is missing and begin to apply it we can let go of the long arduous tasks of fighting, resisting, changing, pushing against, dodging, hiding, running from, fixing, and struggling against this mind in love with attention and control.

Once the idea that 'language is using you, right now' is finally accepted, there is true choice--but not prior to that acceptance. Once our own language is viewed as having power and authority over the addicted minds of the past--in love with attention and control, that transformation becomes possible. Being used by language is not always bad news. If your language is based upon your past beliefs, past negative memories, presumed facts or experiences, or upon the language of some others, you will not be in for a happy ride.

Please do not come to the early conclusion that this is just another 'think a happy thought' book. As you will soon discover, it is much more! When your own voice of authority or language is recognized and appropriated—and is instructed to work for your benefit--it becomes the tool you use every day to transform your own experience, your own reality. You can then choose to proactively and consciously choose a new point of view. This spoken self-chosen point of view causes your own, self-created language that now creates, to use you, therefore creating your own experience—your reality. This is a creative act. You speak it and eventually your language of authority over your past, creates a void enabling you to transforms your reality and begins to give you the life you have always desired.

We need to begin the process of learning the art of self-empowerment, of remembering who we are and stop trying to overpower others. We need to let go of our need to be validated or recognized as being of worth, or of not having the power to stop this madness of ours and start empowering and validating ourselves and each other? Like being sick and tired of being sick and tired. Sick of being used by others beliefs, others language, therefore asserting that enough is enough being spoken this moment.

The experience of *enough*, like most of what we are taught to believe, is not located out there in attempting to control circumstances or events. Enough is located within the authority of our voices having power over the programmed mind. Enough is created from nothing, already having power, simply recognized and appropriated. In order to get 'enough' speaks of not having enough already. Speaking having enough out loud as a truth from nothing causes your world to shift from attempting to get to enough to enough being present. Don't worry, be patient. I will show you how to acquire this authority.

"It ain't what you don't know that gets you into trouble. It's what you know for sure that just ain't so." © Mark Twain

Chapter Eighteen

Distinctions

Space, Context, Designated Space Phenomenon--Assigned Rules or Agreements Within a Context

Space

Space, as of now, is defined as the nothingness that surrounds us.

Context

This nothingness is located and contained within a context called the universe. This space or context within a context has value, as it contains the potential of being extremely valuable to those who recognize and appropriate it.

Context is what surrounds, or is the container of the space or rules or agreements.

Context is "the parts of a written or spoken statement that precede or follow a specific word or passage, usually influencing its meaning or effect:" © Dictionary.com

Within this book, I use *space* and *context* interchangeably. They both express an idea--something understandable, created by agreement--with language.

Designated Space Phenomenon--
Assigned Rules or Agreements Within a Context

Let's get the term *'Designated Space Phenomenon'* out of the way, so that you can hear what I am about to say: First the definition of phenomenon: "Something (such as an interesting fact or event) that can be observed and studied and that typically is unusual or difficult to understand or explain fully." © Merriam-Webster.

The empty space within a circle or context is utilized by creating, by writing, by thinking or speaking into it, or about it.

Designating or creating rules or agreements then acting or reacting on what is thought, written or spoken. Assigning rules or agreements within the empty space or context, produces the results you created.

For example: by placing two dots and a curved line within the circle--or context--could create either a smiley face or a sad face and you will have created some value: a reaction to the assigned agreements or rules. Two dots and a curved line arranged within the context of a circle create value. Easy.

When these assigned rules or agreements are arranged within a context, they create something that has the potential of adding value to our lives. We can choose to give the assigned rules control, allowing them to add value to our lives, placing ourselves at the effect of certain things. These assigned rules or agreements that we create within contexts silently invite us to embrace what we have created within that context--and it is okay. What is unseen is the unlimited potential contained within the context of this nothing.

What I have discovered is that most rules within contexts are already made up prior to our choosing, so we don't have to create them anew. 'They', the Imperial 'they' assigned the rules and agreements within contexts and all we had to do was agree and enjoy their value. We learned the rules within a given context as we were growing up. We just didn't call them by that name. We thought and then said, 'they' know all the answers. 'They' know what is best for us. An example of this space within a context would be a blank piece of paper with an outline of an animal. 'They' said (designating or assigning the rules) of drawing; "color inside the lines" (the context) of the outline of the animal. We learned the rules--the agreements of paper and pens, crayons, toothbrushes, plates, silverware, clothes, shoes, stoves, refrigerators, doors and we learned how they were to be used to receive their value. The rules of life and the uses and values of things were presented to us and were simply passed down to us, as this is how it is.

A *'designated space'* refers to the rules or agreements that someone else determined to fit within the context that would give us maximum value. For example, the inventor of the toothbrush. Hence; a designated meaning, or application. 'They' said and we agreed, whereupon it became our reality. Throughout this book these two words, assign and designate, are interchangeable.

A toothbrush started as an idea, then it became an object and now it occupies the space within the context of keeping our mouths clean. We understand how it is to be used and of what its value is. Man designated (created) its use by rules and agreement. Therefore 'toothbrush' once placed within the space of our mouths (a context of agreement) became useful. That said, the toothbrush could be said to give something to us, its value. We choose to recognize and appropriate its value.

Let us use the bed as another example. It occupies space within a room; a context. What are the designated rules of agreement for the use of a bed? Sleeping, sex, reading, jumping up and down and reveling in the joy of the pitter-patter of a rainstorm of comfort. Again, we choose to recognize and appropriate the value.

Most of us do not work on our car engines in a bed. Does anyone have four people over for a poker game in their bed? Clean machine parts, or refinish furniture on their bed? So a bed occupies a space within a context containing space or rules of agreement in regard to receiving its given value.

The bathroom, 'They' said that a bathroom (context) is a designated space within the context of a house or apartment for baths, showers, brushing of teeth, primping, doing your business, shaving and sometimes reading. The choice of recognition and appropriation of the value is again present.

Does anyone do his or her dishes in the bathroom? Anyone eat dinner in the bathroom? How about parking your car? Paying bills? Cooking? The bathroom is also a context, which contains space and rules of agreement with regard to value it offers.

Lastly, let's use the refrigerator (context) as another example: 'They said'; this assigned space is for storing perishable foods within the space of its context. Recognizing the value and appropriating it requires a choice.

Anyone store his or her shoes in there? Any books in the refrigerator? How about you favorite CD's or a camera? You get the idea. So a refrigerator occupies space within a context (house or apartment) with rules and agreements being present enabling us to receive the value it offers.

Now this is the true magic. The space within a context is something that has unlimited potential, that of adding tremendous value to our lives. We unconsciously choose to give it control. We allow it to have an effect on our lives, placing ourselves at its effect as it offers up its value. It uses us and it is okay.

Now again, as to designated space. As human beings we are the ones who seem to have a say in the matter of what goes where and what a space is used for. We seem to feel that we have the ability to assign what is to go into a space, or what goes on in that space. But do we? And is it done consciously or unconsciously? For the most part we do not have to choose again as somebody else already chose for us--the designator, the inventor of the toothbrush perhaps. The agreements, the rules are already there. We just use the designated space and it adds the value to our lives. We have a choice, a say in the matter in allowing those spaces and contexts to have an effect on us as we agreed to follow the rules and prior agreements designated to those spaces. Those designated spaces unconsciously serve or use us and that is okay. They have been established as rules that produce positive results within our unconscious mind.

As these simple examples of already assigned or designated spaces within contexts serve us, it is as though they have a voice; they silently speak to us. It is that little voice that tells you a bed is for sleeping or sex or listening to the rain. It's as though the already assigned space within the context has a say in the matter. We just passively agree. We agree to listen to the rules and agreements within contexts and simply allow them to have an effect on us--to give us their value. As an example let us use the bed. We trust the bed (the agreements or rules) to give us the comfort of a good nights sleep. Most of us do not mistrust a bed.

Now, what if we could choose to recognize and appropriate this thing called space before it's been assigned? Could we create a context, create or assign rules and agreements that would alter or transform our lives in such a way as to give us freedom from unwanted meanings, feelings, circumstances, beliefs or thoughts that diminish our lives? I say we can.

Let's look a little deeper. Let us get to the core of how these designated spaces have come to be. Who or what created or designated these spaces within contexts for us and somehow acquired our agreement? How was that done? Inventors. Did the manufacturer of the mattress just 'think it' to themselves? No, they used the gift we all have called language. Said another way, 'they' had to use the spoken or written language to receive our agreement in order for that agreement to exist. Who agrees? Anyone who sleeps on a mattress.

"Nothing is intrinsically valuable; the value of everything is attributed to it, assigned to it from outside the thing itself, by people." © John Barth

Chapter Nineteen

'They Say' Becomes 'You Say'

When language is used proactively and consciously it has within it the power to allow you to choose to create the rules and agreements of the spaces within contexts. When you follow the directions on How to use this Box called 'Something for Nothing' it can open up doors to futures beyond understanding or known knowledge. It is the something you do not know you do not know how to use. Don't get caught up in the trap of understanding this statement. Be open. It is okay to understand it, yet if you stop there you will miss the most incredible opportunity to experience the power you were given at birth--to experience unbelievable control over your own thoughts, meanings, beliefs, feelings, issues and circumstances that unfold in your life. As you continue to read you will discover the how.

As of now, what we have been taught and are being taught now, is that the act of thinking causes speaking. If you take a few minutes to think this through and stop, look, and intently listen for a length of time there is a very valuable premise present. (Remember is school we were taught to stop, look and listen.) If you stop, look and intently listen you will hear and observe the opposite is actually true. I will use the television and other media as examples.

Commercials on television are spoken into our senses of vision and hearing in an attempt to cause us to act upon what the commercials say. The news media also speaks into our spaces or contexts with their agendas. Speaking is the cause; we are at the effect. Agendas and gains are just what is. I am not saying that they are bad or wrong.

To act, to believe, to purchase, to tell another to accept as truth—these can, or may be attempts to use us, to control what we do, think or believe. We allow the commercials to speak into our spaces, using that part of us that they know has tremendous value—our visual and sense of hearing--and our contexts. Simply stated, we are allowing them to program us specifically for their agenda and gain. It takes deliberate, intentional focused thought to grasp the reality that speaking causes thinking and feelings, yet there is tremendous value in grasping it because it is affecting your life in ways beyond your wildest nightmares. As you read on you will develop the ability and the power to correct it.

To complete the example, even mentally tuning the commercials out causes an effect. When we think or feel that we are being used we automatically respond by attempting to block out information or language, building up walls of resistance to the very thing that contains the something that contains the power of controlling your own life. Your voice, your language!

Unbeknown to us, these walls are then carried out into our relationships, carrying along the effect of blocking out much, if not most of our communications. We are at the effect of others speaking to us, which causes most of our thinking. Viewers regurgitate these effects and reactions when speaking to others about what happened or what 'they' said.

"The single biggest problem in communication is the illusion that it has taken place." © George Bernard Shaw

Those in power speak into our listening, our space, our contexts, all in an attempt to cause thinking (assigning or designate rules and agreements.) Therefore our speaking to others, therefore causing the realities we experience. We actually pay to be told what to think. We are allowing those with an agenda for personal gain to create our realities. Why? Remember in the beginning of this book I stated: Thinking for yourself is difficult, sometimes hard.

Now, what if it was possible to turn the tables on the language that is using us, that 'thing' in love with attention and control we have allowed to have power over us? Could we cause thinking by our own speaking, therefore shifting the reality we experience?

When the spoken language is recognized and appropriated as the cause of thinking, where there is a proactive action, another element of potential value that is mostly overlooked appears and it is called listening.

"Beware of false knowledge; it is more dangerous than ignorance." © George Bernard Shaw

Chapter Twenty

The Power within Listening

Our listening is also a context or space. Please be patient, I am getting to the explanation of all these examples of our body parts being contexts, as it is a corner piece to the puzzle. As of now I assert that your listening is full of past hearings. The past listens, you hear. You hear from your past. You understand listening. Not bad, not wrong, it just is. We react to language instead of hearing what is said. True listening is heard into the space of nothing. With practice and time it is possible to shift from reacting to others speaking to the proactive conscious choice of listening. When this is accomplished, the experience of listening is present, just as it was prior to understanding listening. Some call this the space of no mind or enlightenment. There is no need to go to the mountain or sit with your legs crossed for hours and I will share this discovery as we continue on.

A trip down memory lane is in order here as there is value in this remembering. Some time ago in the past, prior to understanding listening, we experienced listening. Many firsts are located within those moments. The sound of a word, a parents voice, the sound of a bell, a laugh, a giggle. Music, television, a horn honking, loudness, quiet, the singing of a lullaby or maybe someone crying. As we grow the moments change as do the sounds we hear. First moments and memories make an impression on us both mentally and physically as we begin to make choices, judgments and decisions based on those moments forming habits of thinking. Many of these choices are 'unconsciously made' based on sounds, the language we hear, experiences we are present to and the beliefs we are exposed to.

We form likes, dislikes, preferences and opinions, which habitually form our realities and our points of view. It is the words 'unconsciously made' that I want to address. As a person becomes conscious, these habits of thinking made in our past still govern and sometimes control our present lives and there is an anomaly present and it is called our listening. This anomaly has power, the power to appropriate, to create. Listening is following and experiencing the sound---it is hearing with a purpose. Good listening is built on three basic skills: attitude, attention, and adjustment.

*** Some examples of good listening habits are:

1. Listening for valuable ideas.
2. Listening with the mind, not the emotions.
3. Concentrating.
4. Staying present.
5. Adjust their style of listening to the speaker's words.
6. Listening for the facts that support the speaker's ideas.
7. Desire to learn something new, even though complicated.
8. Listening for important and valuable information.
9. Attempt to understand the speaker's point of view.
10. Think about what has been presented and reflect on the message.

*** Some examples of bad listening habits are:

1. Listening to criticize the speaker's voice.
2. Finding fault or Disagreement.
3. Becoming distracted.
4. Faking attention. Not being present.
5. Listening for facts they already know.
6. Wanting to be entertained.
7. Tuning out.
8. Become triggered by certain words, becoming emotional.
9. Daydreaming.

These bad habits of listening cause us to relate to people as being things, not context and being right is the reward. This way of listening surmises that our bad listening habits be used for this reward of being right. We miss the opportunity to learn from this speaker as it states we are triggered by certain words, becoming emotional. It is the meanings of the words we are triggered by, not the words themselves.

The good listening habits surmise that there is a better reward, that of gaining understanding, yet it states that a good listening habit is to listen with only the mind, not the emotions. This way of listening surmises that our good listening habits be used for this reward of gaining understanding. It is also stated that we will miss the opportunity to learn from this speaker if we listen with our emotions.

What if there was a way to listen and receive a reward more valuable than being right or gaining understanding? Something that would allow you to experience listening as a creative tool under your supervision?

Let me explain. Viewing our listening as a context or space allows us to choose what we would like to hear. Contexts need rules or agreements to be of value to us, so what if you assigned agreements about what triggered your listening. Could you then listen with your emotions and receive the 'experience' of hearing. We all do this at selective moments. We choose to listen with our emotions, yet only when it is safe to do so. There is a reason for this and I will soon explain it. We listen with our emotions when we hear music as we think it is safe, yet the words within the music are creating thinking, beliefs, feelings, attitudes and more.

Habits of listening to another while viewing as them as being a context opens us up to hearing in present time, minus thinking we already know, in regards to what the person is going to say. Many of us listen while thinking about what we are going to say when there is a pause. This is a memory of listening, understanding listening, not listening experienced as having value. What is available is listening or hearing for the first time. Hearing for the first time has no meanings attached to it. It is simply hearing what is spoken; yet now we have a choice as to the meanings we attach to the words. With this comes the excitement of hearing, of learning something new, of feeling the moments of joy once experienced. For the person doing the speaking, they experience being heard, sometimes for the first time in a long time without the judgment of right or wrong, better or worse. This is, in my opinion, is something of great value that is missing and desired by every human being. To experience this we must let go of the past of 'thinking we already know' (being right) and the goal of listening and understanding heard from our past.

"Have you ever noticed that when you choose to look at something differently, the something you are looking at changes?" Again, this is a paraphrase of Werner Heisenberg's famous Uncertainty Principle.

Chapter Twenty One

Point of View

A Corner Piece to the Puzzle

Throughout the day we use our ability to look from a 'point of view' at will, yet for the most part we do it habitually, unconsciously and tend to overlook the value of this gift and its ability to add tremendous value to our lives. It is a simple conscious, proactive choice we all can make that has the potential of altering the way we experience the world and the people in it.

Now, let me also clear up the concept of "Point of View". We, as humans, all have a point from which we view our life and the people in it. Over time this view becomes 'the truth' for us and it is backed up by our own knowledge, understanding, beliefs, opinions, meanings and direct experiences with regard to the way life is and the way people are. We believe we know that we are right about what we think we know. Most of us are absolutely sure that this is so, seldom giving it any thought or questioning its validity.

This is what we talk about, discussing it throughout the day and into the night. If someone comes along and has a different point of view, we will argue and sometimes fight to convince that person that their point of view is incorrect. Your point of view is the only point of view you can tolerate hearing about. This sad limited reality is how we spend a good deal of our precious lives.

What if there was a way to alter or transform your life and the point of view you seem to be stuck with? It is nothing you have to acquire, nothing to work for or earn--you already have this gift. The only reason that you are not using this gift to your advantage is because you traded it in in order to be right.

Let's use the earth as a way to better understand this idea; 'Point of View.' Here is an example by which we can remember and experience this phenomenon called 'point of view.' Great wisdom is found in being in this world but not of it. I believe it is Bible-based.

A rainbow is a good example of this. When it is viewed from standing on the earth we see an arc, yet when viewing a rainbow from looking out the window of a plane it is often possible to see a circle. Partial view versus whole view.

When sunlight and raindrops combine to make a rainbow, they can make a whole circle of light in the sky. But it's a very rare sight. Sky conditions have to be just right for this and even if they are, the bottom part of a full-circle rainbow is usually blocked by your horizon. That's why we see rainbows not as circles, but as arcs across our sky.

When you see a rainbow, notice the height of the sun. It helps determine how much of an arc you'll see. The lower the sun, the higher the top of the rainbow. If you could get up high enough, you'd see that some rainbows continue below the horizon seen from closer to sea level. Mountain climbers sometimes see more of a full-circle rainbow, though even a high mountain isn't high enough to show you the whole circle.

Pilots do sometimes report seeing genuine full-circle rainbows. They'd be tough to see out the small windows we passengers look through, but pilots have a much better view from up front. © Earthsky

Think of the last time you were getting ready to get out of your car to board a plane. Just as you boarded the plane to take off, you look out the window and distantly remember or picture yourself about to get out of your car just a short time ago. You are now looking from a different point of view. Now as the plane departs and takes flight, more distantly still, you look back again, remembering or picturing yourself about to get out of your car. Another point of view will appear now, somewhat distant than before. Now you are up to 10,000 feet, not quite at cruse level. Look out the window again. It's a different point of view still. Now looking below you see the small houses, the even smaller cars and the tiny people below. The sizes changed, as did your point of view. As you get to 30,000 feet or cruise level, where did the houses, cars and people go? Did they disappear? Automatically, another point of view.

To take the example further, let's pretend the plane is equipped for space travel. Up, up and away and now you can see the earth as a round globe/space/context containing all that is within it. Another point of view. Can we look at the earth as a context that holds all that is, within the whole? A place where things move about, appear and disappear over time. Always changing, always in motion. Just notice how easy this was once your point of view had changed.

Everything on the earth is in motion, ever changing as we view it. Things, houses, people are appearing and disappearing in the blink of the eyes of time. Fires, deaths, births, marriages, divorces, new houses being built, houses rehabbed, torn down, bridges being built, torn down, accidents, miracles, robberies, churches being established from the ground up, people starving to death, books being written, inventions being created, trash being picked up, animals going extinct, animals being eaten, animals being born, rivers flooding, rivers being tamed, etc. All this is happening while we are in our space, plane or car. Can you still remember or picture yourself in your car? Even getting a glimpse is sufficient to get this explanation across. This changing of one's point of view simply happens. We do not have to much put effort into it; it just does it for us if we simply open up and allow it. Points of view can instantly change, without effort, without strain. Now, are you in that world or are you of it? Kind of makes one think about whom we think we really are as we covet our points of view--of being right and thinking we really know.

What if--*just what if*--there was a possible 'point of view' from which we could chose that would allow us to comfortably relate to other people and ourselves that would give us more freedom and access to our true selves? A point of view that would cause us to be less reactive or triggered. To say it another way, what if we could step out of this subjugated box we allowed ourselves to be put in--at the effect of letting others believe they know who we are and what we are capable of?

I assert that there is a point of view, which only takes a proactive, conscious choice along with a little practice and gained insight.

This thing called a 'point of view' has within it tremendous value and great power. It has within it the power to perform miracles, allowing you to access your true potential as a human being and is available simply by becoming aware or conscious of this gift of altering your point of view—and your life will improve beyond measure.

We all have a point of view. It came to you at your birth. Without your knowledge or consent, it was thrown on you by someone speaking language at you or to you. At that point you more than likely were at the effect of this experience. From that 'point of view', you were lost in a sea of words, sounds, textures and as an infant you lacked the ability or power to comprehend, let alone alter or transform this 'point of view'.

As a child you were not consciously looking or choosing; you are too young. 'It', the language thrown on you, into your context, was doing the looking and choosing for you and it has been doing that looking and choosing for quite some time. It is not bad, not good, not right, not wrong, it just is. I am asking you to consider this. Is this point of view capable of allowing you to receive the value I am attempting to present? Does it allow you to accept or receive what I am stating to be a possible truth?

If you will just take a moment and listen to that voice, your point of view, those thoughts that think, whom it is you think you are, you will be able to answer the question for yourself. When looking or listening from a point of view, there are only a few points of view that block this choice of accepting that what I assert is a truth. Examples; is this possible? It won't work for me. You don't understand. Is this person a con? What will I loose? I already know that. Should I leave now? What is he selling?

Most points of views that come into being are negative. Again, not bad or wrong, they just are. The real question is do they add value to your life? Does the point of view that is doing the looking, or listening for you allow you to receive the value presented? One possible new point of view would be; just maybe. That one word 'maybe' just caused your mind to open up to the possibility of what I am asserting as being possible and you now have the power to continue to choose to listen from that new point of view. If you again take a moment to experience, notice and listen to what keeps you from choosing or entertaining this new point of view, you will get a glimpse of who or what is doing the choosing and where the conversation is coming from. It might be your parents, a teacher, a preacher, the television or radio, someone who gave you the short end of the stick, etc. It is your mind in love with attention and control and it only gives you choices from your past.

As I have mentioned prior to now, the major premise of this book and of many of the books I have written are based on a quote I read some time ago.

"Have you ever noticed that when you choose to look at something differently, the something you are looking at changes?"

As I have traveled along the road I call my life, gaining knowledge and understanding through direct experiences, I discovered that this quote could also apply to how we view others and ourselves, so I altered it to:

"Have you ever noticed that when you choose to look at something or someone differently, the something or someone you are looking at changes?"

This choice to look—and transform is within us all.

Many of us view others and ourselves as things--a label or a statistic--based upon what many segments of society bombards us with every moment of every day. A man or a woman, rich or poor, tall or short, happy or sad, lazy or ambitious, married or divorced, skinny or fat, meat eater or vegetarian, working or not working, positive person or negative person, a number, a statistic, strong or weak, smart of not to smart, black or white, judgmental or non, giving or receiving or somewhere in-between these labels. Also right or wrong, speaking the truth or lying, bad or good. It is just the way we seem to be subjugated--to see others and ourselves as labels.

To become consciously aware of this ability we have to transform our point of view requires another simple experiment and a little practice. The experiment: From where you are now, proactively, consciously choose to, and walk outside of your house, apartment or car. Look around and observe where you are. Now look back to where you just came from. You will experience how simple it is to physically and psychologically change your point of view. It may not seem like your entire world has changed, but if you choose to do it consciously, it is still you who has shifted the point of view.

Now let's try the same exercise with only your thoughts. Start from inside your residents and look around you. Mentally, roughly calculate the monetary value of the items you see in your field of view. First in dollars. Then do the same calculation, but from a point of view of how much you care about what you see and to what degree. Now, look from the point of view of whether an item is useable, or not? Could you then look from giving away what you see? Destroying it? Not valuing it? Not caring about it? You see, these thoughts alter the way things show up in our life, your point of view. The next question is: are these your thoughts about what you think and see?

We all have within us this ability, or as I like to call it--a gift of perception we are not using for our highest good. Consciously it is done with purpose, focusing in the now. Unconsciously, it is done habitually from our past without any conscious effort--unconsciously, automatically. This unconscious part of our brain governs most of our choices and is mostly hidden from our view. This gift of perception is the doorway to begin to know and eventually experience what we do not know we do not know. This new knowing has within it the power to alter your view of life when you tap into, recognize and appropriate it over time and practice.

I am going to ask you to set aside this unconscious point of view mentioned above or in order to say it another way, this ineffective way of looking at others and ourselves as things or objects. Now with the gift you have, your gift of choice, I am going to ask you to mentally step into a world you might begin to question: this is the world of maybe, just maybe there is something to be discovered that has been hiding in plain sight.

We are not aware of the power this gift of choice has to offer. It is only available to those who discover it subtle power. If you can be truly present, just notice your minds automatic response to being asked to set aside your point of view. Are there thoughts of resistance or acceptance, guilt or freedom, right or wrong, good or bad, better or worse, fear or calmness? I assert that those thoughts, beliefs and feelings are coming from your past, your past in love with attention and control. You did not consciously choose them. Utilizing this power of simply looking from a new point of view has within it the means of discovering your true power as a human being. Just for a few more pages, I am going to ask you to entertain the possibility that what I have to say is valid and it being based on many direct experiences.

For those of you that are curiously, patiently, trusting me enough to continue on, I would like to invite you to find a piece of paper and a pen or pencil. This will only take a few minutes of your time and if you can grasp the potential of again looking from the following new point of view, I can assure you that you will be amazed.

Use this piece of paper to draw a line around the outer edge of the paper, representing the context or space you occupy within--your house or your apartment, your car or your office. Now within that box draw a six-inch square box to represent another context. Now inside the box draw a stick person in the middle of that box about four inches tall. Now draw small circles inside the context surrounding the stick person. The small circles within the box you drew represent thoughts, issues, meanings, beliefs, past memories, worries, stress, circumstances, feelings, friends, relationships, events, things, and more. For now, just notice that within this drawing that represents you within a context, you are taller, you weigh more than what those 'little' circles represent. You are stronger, bigger.

As you look at the drawing, realize that the stick person

represents you within the context of another context, surrounded by 'little' contents. Get a clear idea of what these words context and content mean. I will address this word 'little' as we continue on and it will become clear to you that you already have the power to transform these 'little' contents into being powerless over you.

An example of "content" is the ideas or words within the context of this book.

Remember a context is: "the parts of a written or spoken statement preceding or following a specific word or passage, usually influencing its meaning or effect."

Again: "the circumstances that form the setting for an event, statement, or idea, and in terms of which it can be fully understood and assessed."

Or; "The set of circumstances or facts that surround a particular event, situation. Something that contains and holds the contents of that something."

The United States is a context that contains all of the states. The universe is a context that contains everything along with heavenly bodies like the earth and the United States are contents within the context universe.

Now, viewing yourself (the stick person) as a context; the small circles you drew within the square surrounding you represent ideas, thoughts, meanings, assertions, situations, issues, beliefs, feelings, memories, worries, stress, circumstances, feelings, friends, relationships, events, things, and more and are all thoughts or words, created using language and can also be said to be contents, so you are surrounded by 'little' contents.

Remember the stick person drawing. You can now free to choose a new point of view, one of seeing yourself as being located 'within' a context, the larger square. Allowing you to look at your life 'from' outside of the subjugated box, or context called your life. This is now a new point of view. You are looking at yourself as located within a context, as opposed to being viewed as being trapped within the subjugated box I mentioned earlier: The box we allowed others to view and interact with us as being a thing or statistic. You are now surrounded by 'little' things, objects, events, meanings, thoughts, beliefs, sounds, smells, circumstances, rules, agreements, feelings and more, located within that context. You are surrounded by the language of meanings, created by that mind in love with attention and power.

This context called your personal space is now the place where those 'little' things—the trifles and concerns, are now located within a context—your box--then not there or might I even say that they disappear or are transformed from time to time? Headaches are and then they are not. Thoughts come and they go. Feeling rise and they fall. Sounds appear and then fade. Meanings surface and disappear. We remember and we forget. People come and they go. Worry enters and then exit. All of this happens within your personal context.

Examples of 'little' things located within your personal context, your box; could be friends, enemies, money, glasses, clothes, wives, husbands, houses, cars, jobs, wisdom, experiences, stress, thoughts, beliefs, doubts, judgments, fears, guilt, boredom, fatigue, low self worth, weight problems, sleepless nights, anger at yourself and others, ailments, past memories, regrets, feelings, sickness, fatigue, lack of focus, worries, youth, teenager, adult, elderly, and even death.

Could this drawing—this stick figure inside a box—surrounded by another context give you some idea of the tremendous value in store for you once experienced? By the end of this reading, you will see with certainty that it will exceed your wildest dreams as to its worth.

The you who is **looking** at the box or context is the real you, the one you have been conned into believing is not the real you. The one you forgot was you. **You are also a context.** You have allowed language spoken by others to create your context--the rules and agreements of the contents within the space of who you are, how you think, how you feel and how you act. These 'little' contents that surround you are saturated with meanings you did not consciously choose to give them, placing you at the effect of many of them, which causes you to think, experience and believe 'they' have power over you. Once you remember, recognize and appropriate the concept of who you truly are as a context, you will be able to transform them into the nothingness they are. You were born from a conception, being a notion, an idea.

If you just take a few minutes and consider this premise that we are context or space, as apposed to being a thing, you will get a glimpse what I am asserting. We are bombarded with propaganda that goes right into the space or context of who we are. The sad part is that we go willingly to slaughter, not really able to figure out what is happening to us. We don't seem to have a choice or a voice loud enough to stop the force of the meanings that permeating our contexts. It is as though our shields are down during an overbearing war being conquered up by an invisible force. Somewhat similar to the Shock and Awe war with Iraq.

"Thousands of geniuses live and die undiscovered - either by themselves or by others." © Mark Twain

Chapter Twenty Two

Things vs. Context
Another Corner Piece

See if you can relate to this from your own point of view. For me it was like this. In my past, my boss did not appreciate my work ethic, my value to the company I worked for. I gave 16 years of my life attempting to be of value and for someone to finally recognize it and promote me. Guess what? They just used me, kept promising me it would come in the future. That future never came. I 'thought' (a belief put in my space when I was not sifting or choosing) they had the power to promote me and they had ahold of the reins of how my life was going to go. The fear of choosing was mine and they knew it. I had a family to support, a house payment, food to buy. Standing up to 'the man' meant being outcast or fired. Looking back, I see many companies still doing exactly that. They keep their employees ignorant to the facts of life. We already have the means to build ourselves up and promote ourselves.

    Now, in time I did stand up and one night I quit and took back control of my life. But wait, there was a huge problem waiting for me on the other side of that choice to quit. I now had to learn how to be my own boss and what I did was amazing. I just replaced the way my boss had treated me and now my own mind treated me that way. It was in my space, as I was still a thing, not yet a context. So, how does one get rid of what is in one's space?

    We have all tried changing it, fixing it, replacing it, talking it out with a shrink, being determined, being committed, promising, bargaining, etc. You get the idea. We are still things. We are not yet contexts.

    Ponder this concept for a moment or two. Stop and look around, listen and to how we as humans address each other. Don't we address each other as things, like man or woman? Mostly we see each other as this box called man or woman. Men are this way; women are that way, right? There are some different characteristics, habits, looks, beliefs, religions, colors, sizes, weights, etc., yet we are locked into this view of human beings. It just is. It is 'the' truth. "The truth shall set you free." Well, how is this working? Do you feel and experience freedom? We believe, we act and react like we are limited by how we see each other because others are locked into 'the' truth.

What if who we really are is a context; "the situation in which something happens or the group of conditions that exist where and when something happens." A space where stuff shows up? If we were context wouldn't 'stuff', like and from the past, keep showing up. Just stop, look and listen.

*** How do we get to this place called 'being' a context?

When you consciously, proactively choose to alter or shift your point of view of yourself and others to being contexts rather than things you will begin to peel away the onion of deception you have been crying over for so many years. If you just took a few moments to consider who you would be without the meanings of stress, worries, doubts, judgments, fears, guilt, boredom, fatigue, low self worth, weight problems, meanings, sleepless nights, anger at yourself and others, ailments, past memories and regrets, then you would see yourself again as living a life with purpose, happy to have arrived at this place you call your life. I heard someone describe this plight we all seem to have fallen into as the years have passed by. I intended to make a huge difference in the world and then I saw something shiny. What happened is that you lost sight of your purpose, your true power. You just forgot.

Well, you now have a Book and a Box where you can choose to consciously, proactively designate this Box to be used for the purpose of placing something unwanted into it. Something that has the potential of transforming all those 'little' things I mentioned previously into nothing, Nothing but a trivia. Once applied, this action will allow you to see those annoyances anew, while slowly reigniting your purpose and re-establishing your true power. Your power is still there, yet over time you have been ripped off, your power has been stolen, squelched by those whose desire is to dominate, control and manipulate. You have allowed the flame of desire to be doused by a plethora of flavored waters poured over those desires.

As I have mentioned previously we have a choice and that is to hold ourselves responsible for that rip off and recognize who has allowed the waters to be poured on those desires and especially why we allowed that to happen. (We refused to think for ourselves). Responsibility meaning owning up to 'what is' minus the meanings that were attached to 'responsibility' in the past, prior to you choosing the meaning. Responsibility is not right or wrong, better or worse, good or bad, heavy, blame, fault, burden, shame or guilt. It just is, as you are context, not a thing.

"A man should look for what is, and not for what he thinks should be." © Albert Einstein.

One of our most basic needs are relationships, to belong. In the words of Baumeister and Leary, "It seems fair to conclude that human beings are fundamentally and pervasively motivated by a need to belong, that is, by a strong desire to form and maintain enduring interpersonal attachments." © Baumeister and Leary.
 Not only to be in a relationship with another, but to be able to personally relate to something, be it a volley ball named Wilson, portrayed in the movie Castaway or a pet animal portrayed in the series Lassie many years ago.
Many of us, through no fault of our own, have felt breaks in that belonging throughout our lives. For some, it is a very traumatic event, for others it is the break up of our first love, the loss of a pet, the loss of a loved one, or a divorce. Logically, most of us understand that this loss or break in belonging is a natural part of life, yet others do not fair favorably during this event. Many go through their life looking, needing to connect with another in the attempt at filling the void left by the loss. Clubs, gangs, religion, organizations, social groups, protesters, causes, books clubs, movies, entertainment, hobbies, sports, work, education, achievements and more all seem to temporarily fill this gap. The results of this misunderstanding is that you had a break in belonging to something.
On the flip side of this example there are certain costs present. It appears when the need of something or someone outside of your self causes an unbalance within. Some of these

costs are: loss of true self, loss of personal power, loss of self control, loss of your chosen purpose, loss of control of your emotions, loss of the ability to express your true feelings and your own thoughts, loss of ambition or motivation, loss of certain desires, or the loss of feelings of excitement or joy…and over time these losses transform some people into being at the effect of the desperate search of needing to please others in order to feel whole and complete. Pleasing others is a great feeling and a wonderful gift to be experienced, yet when it is done in order to feel complete it absolutely cripples the person you truly are.

Needing to fit in is another one of the causes of many disasters in life as we give up whom we are in order to fit in as an individual, and being an individual is frowned upon in many societies. It is as though we have this tribal nature, this needing to belong that drives us to allow others to rob us of out true natures. Almost like the game of 'Whack a Mole.' If we attempt to stay true to ourselves we get whacked down by something or someone demanding that we fit in.

After a year-long stay in Japan, a friend recounts her experience:

"You must conform, in every way. As I walked by the Hitachi Factory in the morning on the way to school, the employees would all be doing their exercises—jumping jacks, the whole nine yards--in their uniforms, chanting. We were expected to do the same at school.

Physical exams were performed, naked, in front of all of the other students. It was humiliating and dehumanizing. That is an integral part of their culture—humiliating and dehumanizing. Above all, we were never to outperform any other student in any way. It was as though we were a bed of nails, and if any nail was higher than the other. It was immediately hammered down.

This was difficult for me as I had blonde hair, blue eyes, sang and played the guitar, got great grades, and was fairly outgoing—as a previously non-Japanese speaker. I wasn't part of the tribe and got a lot of hammering. Becoming fluent actually made things worse. The Japanese culture is famous for their innovations in manufacturing (copying), but not invention or innovation. The trick is to stay below the nail that is higher than the others. Nothing else is rewarded." © Kim Knox

So how does one belong to, and be part of something like a relationship and not loose their true selves? Here is what it takes: By being conscious, proactive, and choosing a point of view that has within it the power to alter how people, issues or things show up in your view. Just for a moment, let us experiment with this gift of proactive, conscious choice and let's use human beings as a starting point. First take a look from a given point of view held by many, one that human beings can relate to. The 'point of view' of being related to as 'things': labels, statistics, wins, losses, weight, money, no money, color, age, actions, talents, words we use, beliefs, justifications, honest, dishonest, education, defenses, openness, intellect, status, married, divorced, single, judgments of good or bad, better of worse.

What might happen if that point of view we have of others was altered; shifting it to viewing them as being context or space, surrounded by thoughts, meanings, feelings, beliefs, things, issues and circumstances? What might be available, that may have been hidden prior to this new way of looking at others and us as context? When we shift from the perspective of viewing the person as being a thing, to viewing them as a context, the thoughts, meanings, beliefs, issues or circumstances are within the context with them (within the box around our stick figure). We are viewing them as being a context contained within a context (the Box) surrounded by 'little' things that is held within a bigger context called their residence.

In the beginning it might look like the 'little' things, meanings or issues are really who the person is within the context, but a closer look will allow you to see that they are just who they are, in their own space or context, along with their issues, meanings, thoughts, beliefs or circumstances, much like ourselves. The evidence that the things, thoughts, meanings, issues or circumstances are bigger than them is located in a point of view, again much like us. Could we simply alter our point of view to; "I am much bigger than the issues, the meanings, the feelings, the beliefs, the thoughts or circumstances?" Use plain old common, sense here. If you look at the picture you drew you will see that they are taller than and weigh more than a thought, meaning, belief, feeling, issue or a circumstance.

From this new point of view, it is though they are

surrounded by issues, meanings, beliefs, circumstances, or thoughts? Context is the space that things show up within, right? Again, I pose the question; are issues, meanings, and thoughts or circumstances us, or are they simply located within the context or space we occupy? Pondering this is sometimes difficult, yet it contains extraordinary value. Remember it is just a point of viewing someone or something.

"Too often we ... enjoy the comfort of opinion without the discomfort of thought." © John F. Kennedy

I will continue to use 'others' in this example, yet it is the same for us. In the past, prior to this new 'point of view', those unwanted things, issues, thoughts, meanings, beliefs, or circumstances were considered as though they were part of them, of being an intimate part of them, having them--being something within themselves they had to fix or change. In that past point of view they had very little power to alter, transform, change or fix what they thought would make them feel better or improve their lives until they fixed or changed them. Somewhat like a broken person attempting to fix a broken person with the same tools that put them in that box. Might there be a faster, simpler, easier way?

Let us ponder something, an issue of sorts, just for practice: Stress. Stress causes immense problems in the body and in the mind. It is often held as the cause of destroyed families, causing among many divorces and sometimes hospitalizations if not treated. Within this new point of view of us being space or context, stress is now in the context with them, not yet separate from them. Think of the stick figure in the box. Stress is inside the box, with them. They might believe or feel like stress is part of them, as they have evidence to prove it. They call it stress. To say it another way, and more accurately, it, the stress has them, even within the same context or space. When the stress is within their context or space and they have the view of themselves as being a thing, the person and the stress are joined as one.

We are now going to shift our point of view from those things or issues having them, to a new point of view: simple acceptance of 'what is' in the space or context. By 'what is' I mean, what could be seen without the labels of blame, shame, fault, guilt, right or wrong, strong or broken, good or bad, better or worse. They are just there in the space or context with those issues, thoughts, meanings, beliefs, issues or circumstances. Most of what is now missing from this point of view are the verbal and mental judgments or meanings of our past. We are just going to hold those at bay for a few moments--to be able to simply take a look at their context from this new point of view. Could stress just be stress, without the meanings and feeling? Why does it feel bad or unwanted, this thing called stress? Answer = Agreement and past meanings! Stress just is.

Now that you have read this example, let's shift the tense from them to including us or we, recognizing the opportunity to personalize it. What if we chose to proactively consciously 'put' the stress within our own context, therefore allowing the stress the space to be where it is, but without the meanings? (Putting it there needs some explanation):

Choosing to put something where it is or what it is causes acceptance of 'anything that is'. It separates the meanings from what is. This is much different than allowing or tolerating, or putting up with. Intentionally, consciously, proactively putting something 'where it is' located or 'what it is' without the past meanings, unleashes the power within, the something you unknowingly gave away. It is being the cause or true choice.

"I have always believed, and I still believe, that whatever good or bad fortune may come our way we can always give it meaning and transform it into something of value." © Hermann Hesse.

This is where the magic starts—where your true power is recognized and appropriated. Giving meaning to life as opposed to expecting life being subjugated to give you meaning. Asking not what life can do for you, but what can you do for life? If you take just a moment to think, you will see life really does not give a damn; it just is; yet we live our lives as thou it does.

This realization places you at cause, meaning I am responsible, without the past meanings placed on being the cause or responsible. Meanings like blame or shame, guilt, bad, right or wrong, heavy or uncomfortable. Being the cause, like being responsible, just is. Remember the seven billion people across the world, including us, as we are all making up the meanings, the truths, the realities we experience in our world, our lives. You now have a voice, a choice. The meanings 'they' bombard us with every day or you choose to make it up anew. You now have a say in the matter of your life as to what everything means. You are at cause and responsible. Again, remember the elephant metaphor, small bites.

Again I repeat, our 'thoughts of the past' are in love with attention and control. They rebel against us--against who we really are, the chooser. What we do not realize is that we have the power to simply, consciously, proactively choose what is. The meanings of what is were invented by others, and we accepted those meanings. We blindly chose to adopt those meanings—those beliefs--as truths of our own and now we will soon be able to choose to have them be nothings, nothing but a trivia and have them transform.

This choice to have stress just be stress within ourselves as context allows it to simply 'be' within our context or space. It is not good, bad or unwanted, it just is. Using your gift of choice when addressing this thing called stress and assigning it a new meaning of 'what is' will be revealed in the next chapter. This is where your true power starts to be experienced.

A bit of wisdom I gained during my life goes like this. Anything or something you can allow the space to just be, that something; for example stress, either leaves you alone, or to say it another way, whatever is in your space transforms or disappears. Might the stress leave the space without the past thoughts, meanings, beliefs or feelings that something was either bad or wrong or that it was something that was not wanted? Remember; what your resist, persists.

I say it will and does take some verbal and mental practice along with developing the patience to allow the stress the space to just be. We live in a world of dualities. In order for relaxation or ease to be present we must allow stress the space to just be, minus our past thoughts, feelings, meanings and labels. Viewing others and us as contexts creates the space for the stress to just 'be' as opposed to viewed people as being a thing. This ability will become clear as you read on.

Seeing ourselves as context or space allows the stress and the relaxation or ease to co-exist, both experiencing the space to just be. Once we choose to have stress be what it is without the meanings, it can be just that, stress. As 'stress' looses its meanings and overpowering voice over us, it becomes diminished and is transformed.

The same principle applies to many other things I have mentioned earlier. A simple example of this is anything you choose to look at. A pencil does not bother you or upset you, aside from having to be sharpened, because there are not too many negative meanings attached to it. A phone is another example. It is just a phone, yet we can attach meaning to it, as in anticipating a call from a loved one, or not wanting it to ring during certain times. If a person is in business, we can attach meanings for it not ringing if it is one of the sources of our profit.

The world and all its troubles are good examples. What might happen if a person just chose to have the earth and all of its troubles to just be and then chose those meanings for themselves? Another way to look at this is that the world really is the way it is, and it is the way it isn't, so meanings are generated by each of us, both individually and globally.

"We cannot solve our problems with the same thinking we used when we created them." © Albert Einstein

Chapter Twenty Three

Agreement

Using the example of the point of view of seeing yourself and others as contexts, something is missing and it is called agreement. This is a pitfall we might fall into. Is it needed? Is it missing? Who has what is missing? Where is it located? If we get to the core of this thing called agreement we need to look at what it comes from, it's essence. Isn't it also language? Now, who has language? You do, your voice. Yes you do, if you choose to recognize it and appropriate it. So what if you spoke to yourself instead of to another and received agreement, as though you were speaking into your own listening. What might this action cause? Loneliness at the beginning, I agree. Maybe a little narcissistic thoughts or tendencies. We might not be comfortable giving or asking ourselves for agreement, yet we do it unconsciously all day long, so there is nothing to acquire.

We choose to give ourselves agreement to eat, sleep, go and play, work, watch tv, read, study, relax, call a friend, debate, argue and so on. We give ourselves agreement to do it all. In the past might you have been looking outside of yourself for this something you already had, not knowing there might there be another way?

What if you tried another little experiment: speaking to another as though you were speaking to yourself, speaking in such a way as to add value to their lives. Giving them exactly what you want or need to accept, as in the idea that a Box called 'something for nothing' being viewed as having tremendous value. What if you ran up against some resistance to this belief you have of 'something for nothing' being of tremendous value that is not immediately accepted. Imagine then if you held that resistance as your own resistance. Picture this situation as though it were a mirror into which you could see, hear, feel and experience your resistance, letting you know that acceptance is missing. In Whom? In you. What would most of us do? Push harder? Try another approach? Give up? I did, and I did it for a long time.

Here is what I eventually did. I took responsibility for the resistance I was experiencing within the space of a conversation. As I was attempting to share a truth I had discovered, if I noticed resistance showing up, I began to hold myself responsible for unknowingly creating or causing the resistance. As I viewed 'causing it' without adding blame, fault, right or wrong, good or bad past meanings, it eventually transformed into resistance simply being what it is without the past meanings. It lost its power, and its control within the conversation. It left the space, disappearing into the space outside of the context, into nothing. What showed up was acceptance of the idea.

Then I questioned, what is missing if resistance is present? Answer: acceptance. What if you could place the resistance into the box called 'Something for Nothing' that would transform that something (resistance) into nothing--Nothing but a trivia? You can, and the 'How to work the Box' will clarify it. More patience in needed here. You have come this far, many won't.

As you continue this experiment you will eventually receive the acceptance you are attempting to receive from another--within yourself--at a very deep level. Placing something in the Box is an example of the power of taking away and assigning other meanings to something. These are meanings from your past thoughts, beliefs, feelings and actions. When you discover that you have this power over your own life right now, this phenomenon can be true in your future. You will become your own master, the captain of your own ship. You will have a say in the matters of your own life, your own thoughts, your own meanings, your own feelings and your own actions. The results are simply balance, clarity and confidence.

Your choice is to take the point of view that we, as humans beings, are all context--not just things. A space where things, thoughts, beliefs, meanings, issues and people show up. At that point, we can truly hold ourselves responsible for what is in our space or context without all the chatter of it being bad or good, better or worse, right or wrong.

Responsible means choosing to view others and ourselves as context or space rather than that of being a thing. Using some of Werner Erhard's little sayings, 'what is, is', 'what ain't, ain't' and 'what is so, is so', and 'so what?' keeps the skewed meanings at bay. This is to include not only the beliefs we all have but also the beliefs that were placed upon us. This also includes feelings such as guilt, shame, worry, stress, and judgments that may possibly be in our spaces.

There are also various personalities that we have allowed into our lives, which either support us or diminish us. Rather than being victims at the effect of others and their shenanigans or manipulative games, we can own up to the realization that we allowed this or people's language into our space or context, and if we do not want it or them in our space we now discover that we have the power to transform it, remove it, or them.

This is who we really are. We can choose to hold ourselves responsible for what is in our space or context. Holding yourself responsible also has within it unconsciously assigned meanings from the past, placed there by the collective unconscious. On the whole, these meanings and beliefs were made up by others, which most are not aware of. The concept of responsibility is basically held by many as meaning shame, heavy, good or bad, difficult, a burden, guilt, fault or blame. From the new point of view of these concepts simply being within your space or context, responsibility is simply 'what is so' without the thoughts, beliefs, meanings and feelings of your past programming. You are just being responsible. From this place you can choose to respond with your truth or not, as you are no longer at the effect of the language of others.

Those who want to attack you, criticize, blame, guilt you into submission, shame or burden you are just stuck in their past programming. When those statements are heard as, 'what is' or there is no judgment, no right or wrong, there is no having to defend yourself, as you do not have any meanings attached to what they say or do. You will soon discover when you apply these principle statements such as those mentioned, they will just bounce off of you, having no effect on your peace of mind. I have learned through direct experiences a simple response to the language of others that causes no resistance within. It is simply the words 'no thank you.'

"Have you ever noticed that when you look at something or someone differently, the something or someone you are looking at changes?"

Think once again, Looking is the amazing gift of perception and it has great power when utilized consciously and on purpose.

I am going to ask you to just take a few moments to look at everyone this way-- at everyone in your world. Now, if possible, again look at yourself from this different point of view, just for this moment of consideration. No gimmick, no pressure, no have to. Just a simple choice to use your innate talent to simply take a look at this moment in time. I want you to choose to alter your point of view from seeing people and yourself as labels, but rather to see them as being their own contexts, occupying spaces, surrounded by contents; simply words with meanings. Utilizing this ability, which is already part of who you are takes a little practice. Think of it as a muscle, a part of your brain that has slowly slipped into atrophy. In time, the results of proactive, conscious choosing to look at people and things from this new point of view will begin to quiet your mind and give you a sense of peace beyond understanding that will emerge from within. In time, your trials will become a part of your past, and lightness will replace the weight of the issues you have attempted to deal with from your past point of view.

Please be patient. I will not leave you without the solutions.

*** Walkabout. Enjoy ***

Some time ago I met a friend, a man, a decent man, a man who had done something in his past that caused him much regret. He would speak of it once in awhile in confidence as the pain he felt was deep within his soul. One day he mentioned it again and I painted him a picture with the words I spoke to him. He was a polite man, a man with a high regard for the feelings of others, so he allowed me to quietly enter his patterns of thought. I suggested to him that he place this issue in the back of his pickup truck the next time it surfaced to haunt his present experience.

His demeanor was of kindness as he responded to my suggestion with a simple "Humm, I will think about that." In time we would see each other, say out hellos, and then one day he mentioned the suggestion I made to him, the one he said he would think about. I responded with excitement, hoping for another opportunity to share something I had discovered as magical with him. We both laughed at the silliness of the thought of placing it in the back of his truck, but his response caught me off guard. He mentioned to me that the issue was actually staying in the back seat, yet it did scream once in awhile trying to get his attention. We both then related it to children being on a long vacation drive, being bored and wanting attention. Again the laughter kept the interaction light, so we discussed the options available in regards to these children (past issue). We could tell them to shut up and be quiet, but that did not align with who my friend was, so we came up with a different solution. I suggested that he now picture a trailer hooked to the back of his truck, one he could drag behind him. "Maybe you could put that issue in the trailer when it comes up," I suggested, knowing he was open to the possibility.

"I will give that some thought" he quietly responded.

Some time passed before I saw him again and he came up to me and told me that he had been picturing the trailer behind his truck as we had talked about. "You know, a funny thing is happening when I do that. The memory of it seems to be getting lighter for some reason." I told him that I understood the reason and I then asked him if he wanted to experiment with it some more. With a curious glance he said; "Sure, it can't hurt. What do you have in mind?" he said with an accepting smile.

"Would you be willing the disconnect the trailer and let it go?" I questioned him every so softly.

"Humm, that is an interesting thought. I will try that." That was what he did and over time he did disconnect the trailer, releasing with it the meaning he had attacked to the issue of his past and he was freed from its grasp.

"Create your future without a past. © Werner Erhard. or "Create your future from your future not your past." © Werner Erhard.

Chapter Twenty Four

Unconscious Choices

What is this thing called an unconscious choice? It is passive in nature, automatic, quite like a habit of; "Doing the same thing over and over again expecting to get different results." © Albert Einstein and this action is called insanity. We, as humans, are like machines, programmed every moment of ever day to do this or do that, 'in order to' get this or to get that, 'in order to' be happy. In order to become rich. In order to get our parent's approval...in order to get people to like us; In order to _____. You fill in the blank. In order to is not bad or wrong, yet if you take a few minutes and study its assumption, in order to is stating that there is this something that is missing that we simply have to get.

Stating that this something is outside of us, just beyond our reach, we are stuck in the beliefs and feelings of needing this or that in one of the richest countries in the world. What if? Just what if we are unconscious, lost and behind schedule? Could we wake up, find our way and make up for the lost time? How, you might ask?

I say this. 'In order to get' is actually the problem. Aren't we at the effect of the reality we see and the language we hear and repeat? Wouldn't this be considered a 'lack' consciousness? Having to earn, having to learn to deserve, or having to do this or that 'in order to' get? Within that statement is something we may not be aware of. It states that we live in a world of scarcity and that something is obviously missing. Therefore we must spend as much time as it takes—even if it is our whole life--trying to find or get the something that is missing.

Where might this disabling language have come from? Could it have been thrown upon us, spoken by others in our past as a moralistic, suffering, struggle--a perverted way of being? Might it have been spoken to us as 'the only truth', the only point of view, or spoken by those who had a different point of view demanding that we conform to it? Might this have happened before we became aware of having a choice or having the courage to stand up against those big people? Might we have unknowingly given away this something that could protect us from others?

Having language thrown upon us means that language has been spoken into our inner space or context. Whereupon, we were at the effect of language and started thinking and acted on being treated as things, like a machine. We were no longer alive within our own contexts. We believed exactly what was thrown on us. We became accustomed to being seen and treated as a thing or machine, which could be programmed into doing the bidding of those we allowed to be in charge. Was there an 'in order to' attached to this way of thinking, acting, feeling and being thrown on us? I say there was and it is being done to us today, even as I write.

This 'in order to' get is like a virus on steroids, constantly sucking the true power and life out of human beings. Some may label it as ego, religion, government, technology, drugs, competition, progress, etc., yet it all boils down to one thing: something is missing and we must find it 'in order to' survive. Let me pose a possibility, a story I like to share with those who might ask about this premise.

Long, ago, there once lived a fish. This fish swam within an elite school surrounded by all the embellishments of knowledge deciphered from understanding. His colleagues 'they' spoke of this thing called water as though once understanding was found, the finder could live the rest of one's life in peace.

As this fish solemnly dedicated himself to the task at hand, he quickly advanced through the gradients of understanding. He spent all his waking hours searching for this thing he had heard his colleagues speak of, the understanding of this thing of called water 'in order to' live his life in peace. The searcher became who he thought he was, a searcher.

Then one day while diligently in pursuit of his quest, he met a few fish along the path of his migration. As he stopping for a moment of rest, they felt his intensity, became curious and asked him about his purpose. "I am on a mission seeking the understanding of water so that I may live in peace." They all blew a few bubbles of empathy and wished him good luck as they were also in search of the understnding of water.

As he continued on his path of tireless inquiry, he met

another fellow searcher. As the two exchanged pleasantries, speaking in the bubbles of fish talk, he found that they were also on the same quest. They both spoke of their discoveries, of the numerous places where the understanding of water was not located, expounding in detail in regards to the lack of understanding they had encountered, yet neither spoke of experiencing any success in finding this illusive understanding of water they were in search of.

In a moment of discovery and reflection, they looked at each other, each seeing the water surrounding the other, yet could not see the water that surrounded themselves. In an amazing insight of validation, each saw their reflections and both thought they now understood that this thing called water was-- located outside of them.

As for unconscious fish, they are now on our menus.

Within the next moment a bright flash of insight appeared and suddenly each fish dropped this thinking that they knew (swam into the space of not knowing what they did not know) and breathed in the water that had surrounded them for the length of both of their lives.

The instant discovery of this thing called water transformed them as they experienced the wonderful delight of swimming in the water for the very first time. Once they both experienced the water they saw that one thing they had spent their lives looking for 'in order to' live in peace was not located in understanding.

As they both took a moment to bathe in this discovery, they looked back. They could now see that the thing that they had spent their whole lives looking for was, at all times right in front of their eyes, surrounding them, constantly accessible, yet others had lead them to believe that 'in order to' live in peace the understanding of water had to be found.

They were now able to experience this thing called water, knowing they knew it was what supported them and allowed them to breath and live the rest of their lives in peace. They thought they had completed their life quests.

A slimy sly smile crept in on each of the fish as they had discovered this thing called experience as opposed to understanding that others spoke of as being so valuable. They now knew that they knew, but then another question appeared.

Now what? If I am not a searcher, who/what am I?

"If you have inner peace, nobody can force you to be a slave to the outer reality."© Master Sri Chimmoy.

Transformation is similar to this following example. Once enlightenment is experienced the things and issues in life are basically the same, yet you are viewing life from a new point of view, that of everything being contained within. As portrayed in movies like: The Karate Kid, where his student is disciplined to be in the moment by repeating: "wax on, wax off." Zen Masters are said to chop wood and carry water even after enlightenment is experienced because everything is being generated or coming from within.

The following partial text excerpts are as taken from the Editorial, © Kang Maike of Zen Dirt. "Do each task we do with the fascination and wonderment of a beginner. The key to enlightenment is to be mindful of everything we do all of the time. The key to enlightenment is to have a beginner's mind while doing the common things that we are already doing. It is almost like a child doing things for the first time, as they are often amazed at the little things we take for granted each day. Let us not take things for granted anymore. Be mindful, be truly in each moment, do not over-analyze."

We are enlightened beings, spirits in search for the same thing, the water, the language and the experience of peace. Must we spend our whole lives listening to, reacting to and giving attention to the mind which is in love with attention and control, or listening to those who profess that this something is found outside of ourselves, only to discover it is not? Could we choose to give up the search for what is surrounding us? Couldn't we simply recognize it, appropriate and develop it simply by speaking our own language from a point of view of power over the chatter of the mind filled with the past, in love with attention and control? Wouldn't the conscious, proactive choice of the assertion of putting it there, (the mind of past in love with attention and control) within the context or space of whom we already are, allow this new point of view to return us to our true selves?

In regards to this choice of being responsibly, at the cause of our own lives rather than being at the effect of things, beliefs, meanings, issues and other's language. Would the act of putting 'what is' within our contexts shift us from the mind of past having us to us having the mind of past? Picture it like a little circle, a 'little' content. Perspective. Point of view. Who is bigger? Could you now speak to the mind of past as being nothing, Nothing but a trivia?

Being responsible for the proactive, conscious choice of putting something where it is returns you to your true power, causing you to be in control of what is. You are choosing to be responsible for it being where it is, without all the past meanings of good or bad, right or wrong, better or worse. It is just where it is and what it is. As silly as it may sound, do this with everything within your context. When 'understood' this subtle notion has some value. It is the experience of control and power over it I am asking you to stretch for. Experience is gained from taking action, allowing the experience to transform your thinking. Once this is experienced you will know who you are. It is the same with people. Choose to have them be the way they are. Guess what? They are the way they are. Again, without all the meanings, the past judgments of good or bad, right or wrong. Choose to treat them, as being context and the experience will transform your thinking.

You are now at true choice to consciously, proactively purposely attach meanings of your own words or the words of others or not. This spoken action returns you to your true power, choice and control over your past, your past in love with attention and control. Once this something (our voice of authority over our past) is recognized and freely appropriated, this process begins to transform you. Or would we choose to continue life as the unenlightened fish, on the menus for others to feast upon? I intend to dine on life, not to be dined upon. Might you join me for a lovely dinner at 6:00pm?

"I'm not a genius. I'm just a tremendous bundle of experience." © R. Buckminster Fuller.

Chapter Twenty Five

The Power of Choice

"Every man builds his world in his own image. He has the power to choose, but no power to escape the necessity of choice." Ayn Rand

In the beginning, prior to being spoken, language came from nothing. The power of pure choice comes from nothing, no past and no future. It is made in the moment of now. Yet, few choices are made from this moment of now. It is usually something that we are unconscious of that does the choosing. It is of this something that I would like to expound upon.

To choose is a proactive act if it is made from nothing. That state is creative at its very nature. To make a choice from a past memory is the past making the choice, not you. To choose from fear is the fear making the choice, not you. To choose from hoping, hoping is doing the choosing, not you. To choose from any kind of lack, lack is choosing, not you. To choose from boredom, guilt, stress, meanings, worry, doubt, anger, those feelings or thoughts are the ones choosing, not the real you.

You might think, well naturally, that is who I am. My assertion is that those things are not the real you. It is whom you believe yourself to be that has gathered layer after layer of confusion, doubts, fears, powerless, sickness, labels, judgments, hatred, cons, tricks, mistrust, and lack. All of these thoughts are backed up, evidenced by your past understanding of those thoughts, and therefore giving them attention and control, giving them meanings.

It is the programmed machine regurgitating information of past we believed that was spoken by others, as they convinced, acted and pretended, all in an effort to convince us to believe that 'they' or it knows who we are. This is where 'in order to' is located and can be seen and recognized for what it really is. It, this mind of past, that you believe you are, has convinced you that this is truly who you are.

Illusions must fall and truth be known, this illusion is deathly afraid of being seen for what it really is, a powerless illusion pretending to be all-powerful and all controlling. Its biggest fear is that of loosing control of the you it has convinced you that you are. It, this mind of past in love with attention and control continues to con you into believing something is missing. Thinking that this something must be found 'in order to' be happy or satisfied. It is terrified of being seen as what it is, so it convinces you that you are what it is, as it the one who is not whole and complete. Who you are is already whole and complete. The mind is the one that deals in lack, always seeking, always in search of the something that is missing and thinks it is located outside of itself. Like the fish to water, it continues the search for 'understanding' being whole and complete, and convincing all who would listen that completeness is located outside of ones self.

When you purposefully practice looking from the point of view of being a space or a context, you will see or hear the thoughts, meanings, beliefs and those things or issues that have taken up rent free residence in your space.

Once these little annoyances or issues are seen from the point of view of them being in the space or context of who you are, your real power is available to deal with them. They, those little annoyances or issues are just thoughts you have. You gave them power by one simple thing. Your voice! Or if you want this to take a lot of work, struggle and effort, try your thoughts. Ever try and tame or control your thoughts with thoughts? It is possible, yet there is a faster simpler way.

There is a little secret being withheld from you by those who are doing the dining on you.

You might take a few weeks to decisively look at what I am about to say. Look at this from different points of view if you must, but please study it intently. Reflect seriously on it like you were digging for a one-pound bar of 24k gold that is located in this insight. Tremendous value is located in this insight.

"You are always free to change your mind and choose a different future, or a different past." © Richard Bach

This little secret that has been withheld from you is this: speaking causes thinking in the world we now live in. The articulation of words are spoken into the space of something that is invisible, is a thing of no supposed value called nothing, while nothing is very expensive to purchase. 'They' say that and they act upon it as of now. Enormous amounts of money are spent on Super Bowl ads. According to The Wall Street Journal, a basic, 30-second ad for Super Bowl XLIX costs a whopping $4.5 million. It is delivered into the space of something we do not value, as it is nothing or something that is unseen.

So, if this 'nothing' is so valuable, why, oh why does it seem to be difficult to acquire? Why do we resist its presence? Buddha is said to have spent much of his lifetime sitting on a mountaintop in the attempt to arrive at this experience of enlightenment, nothing or the quieting of the mind. What did he know that we don't? What and why are these secrets kept from humanity? Might it be that anyone can create the quietness or nothingness from nothing? Boggles the mind, this creating from nothing, but we will see.

But wait--is there a shortage of this thing called nothing? Like the fish in the water, isn't it everywhere, always available, always accessible, always present, always giving? Doesn't it support us, giving us the gift of breath? Could it be that this thing called space or context is also right in front of our eyes? Are we, like the fish, searchers for what is everywhere yet always seeking it? Are we on the menu? What are those who know the secret feasting on? The answer is within the invisible, unseen, unconscious or subconscious mind. And why do we continue to make this feast available to those who intend to feed upon us? So we don't have to think, and therefore do not have to speak for ourselves.

The act of speaking is choosing to create one's life from the space of nothing, the something that is unlimited. What does it take? The conscious, proactive choice of recognizing and appropriating your own voice of authority over the mind of past.

With practice, this choice will result in you experiencing the power within your own voice to transform whatever content is unwanted within your space or context.

"Sometimes one pays most for the things one gets for nothing." © Albert Einstein.

I say we are on the menu and until we wake up to this fact and start making conscious, proactive choices and act on the realization that the time is now, we will always be on their menus. Werner Erhard once said in a seminar I attended, that life comes at us 'point blank,' yet we think and act as if there is another life we get to wake up into and begin to experience our true potential and power.

I have come to a place in my life where I now experience the daily knowledge of this moment. Erhard also coined a few phrases such as, "this is it" and "what is, is, and what ain't, ain't." These clever witticisms are now profundities that permeate my life. Understood, they have some value, yet when experienced they are the breath of a life which is lived through direct experiences creating knowledge.

"For time and the world do not stand still. Change is the law of life. And those who look only to the past or the present are certain to miss the future." © John F. Kennedy

Discovering who you are requires a willingness to let go of first base to steal second base. You're taking a risk. You are looking and choosing to step out into the nothing between the bases. Prior to writing the books I have written, I absolutely knew I could not do it. I wanted to but knew I could not, as I had attempted it on numerous occasions. That absolute knowing kept me in a grip of despair with regard to my writing for too many years, as I thought my fears and doubts were real. It was not that I didn't take the risks, as when I did I unknowingly stepped into the space of nothing. Each time I stepped into this nothing it triggering the meanings of past where the notions of fear and doubt were patiently lurking. Relentlessly, they were ready to ambush my attempts by attaching negative meanings and unexpected feelings to my thoughts, my efforts and even my progress.

Then one day Lulu a friend of mine and I were discussing this phenomenon regarding language having the power to transform issues. From my point of view she was a creative artist and a prolific writer, as she had shared some of her drawing and writings with me. She also saw something in me as a writer from her point of view. We had heard it spoken of in seminars we had attended and both of us had witnessed this phenomenon personally. As we discussed the possibility of it being a game we could play, we reached an agreement.

We consciously, proactively created a context, a game, creating it from nothing but our speaking. This game was to consist of agreements or rules that we also created from nothing. We just made them up. We were going to attempt to transform each other's writing issues by using the power of language spoken into each other's space or context or notably the subconscious mind.

The Game: we were going to speak to each other based upon what we could see in each other as our truth, our points of view. The excitement and fear were palpable for us both as we were willingly embarking on an adventure into the dark unknown of both our past beliefs, broken dreams, failures and disappointments.

The rules:
1) We agreed to commit fully to the game, to play full out with abandonment, being unreasonable and audacious with each other and ourselves.
2) The second rule of the game was to be willing to let go of our own rightness and points of view we held about ourselves regarding the issue of being writers.
3) We also agreed to allow the words spoken to each other to be followed with a simple 'thank you' even though neither of us might have believed the other person's words. This meant we would do our best to not let our mind's desire to be right get inside this game by making the other person's words or point of view wrong.

Her amazing talents as a writer and an artist were blatantly obvious to me, yet from her past point of view she could not see or accept what I saw as an obvious truth. Then she spoke of my talents as a writer from her point of view. I too could not see what she saw or accept it from where I looked, as it was also viewed from my past thoughts of which I spoke of often in frustration.

As we played the game, we discovered that we could see each other's ability as a writer from a different point of view. We had both been standing on the precipice of understanding, giving attention to our pasts in love with attention and control, yet the agreed upon value of understanding our pasts lacked the real juice of action and results.

Each day, every day for about 30 minutes we would play the game, speaking our truths to each other about the other. At first it was an awkward conversation, yet over time it became just like a game, as it was fun to play. Our attention and focus was on each other's talent and we got to complement and acknowledge each other to our hearts content. The rule of saying, 'thank you' became a very empowering tool as we both finally experienced being heard. The insights and discoveries of being told that you are a writer were extremely rewarding, as we were soon to discover we had both been trying to get what we already had. We had both resisted believing it for too many years and resisting the belief continued to give it power. "What you resist persists."

After we had played this game for about three weeks I received a call from Lulu. "I am a writer" came from the shrill in her voice. The game was now alive with power and accomplishment. She had now experienced being a writer. We both began to laugh as she had come to this place of discovering the obvious. What does a writer do? They write. She began to write with a fevered pitch generating her first book within the next two months. As of this date she has written about seventeen books. One of them is called Ruminations by Lulu M. Flatt, which I highly recommend, as it truly showcases her amazing talents. It can be found on Amazon.com.

I, on the other hand, was still stuck in my past beliefs. Over the next week doubts began to creep in as to the possibility of also tapping into this experience of being a writer. As our conversations continued I struggled to maintain the intensity of the game, and relied heavily on the fact that experience was indeed transferable. I was beginning to understand the potential power contained within this game we had created and was excited about sharing my findings.

That next Saturday I was at a meeting I lead and I made a statement to the group regarding what I had just discovered. My statement was: "If you want something, all you have to do is recognize it and appropriate it, as it is free." As bold as the statement was, I was beginning to experience the possibility of it and I wanted to share this discovery with the group. After the meeting was over a friend of mine said something very important to me, even to this day. He suggested that I should learn to 'blog'. Now the word itself was not the gift he gave me, it was the effect it had on me at that time. He was aware of my desire to write and he thought blogging would give me the desired experience of writing. Blogging was one of those things that was both beyond my understanding and beyond my reach.

Upon arriving home I fired up my Mac to look at the possibility of blogging and again came face to face with the experience called being dumbfounded by what I didn't understand. At the moment of experiencing this feeling of not knowing how to blog, the experience of not knowing how did not mean anything. It vanished into nothing. The 'wanting' to be a writer disappeared, turning instantly into writing. Poof! Not knowing how no longer had any power over me. As I reflected on that moment of transformation, I became aware of the power of another's point of view. Not knowing how was now devoid of the meanings I had given it, it just was. Experiences like that catch my attention. I want to know what happened and why did it have such an effect on me. As time has gone by, I now have another bit of valuable insight into the ticking of the human mind. That one simple suggestion spoken out loud to me in that moment changed the direction of my life.

I called Lulu and shared my discovery of experiencing being a writer. We both celebrated the success of the game. Lulu then shared each of her experiences as she progressed, learning through trial and error the workings of the publishing world. Later on, after I caught up with her, I too began to learn about this world of publishing and we again began to learn from each other. I now knew that the game Lulu and I had played was a powerful catalyst that causes opening up to the power of accepting another's suggestion or support. The amazing thing about this is that some months later, my friend who suggested I learn to blog, wrote his first book. The Weekend Warrior by Jens Tobias. Over the next seven months I wrote six books.

Speaking into the space of nothing has the power to alter a life in a negative or positive way. I had studied this for many years. I had read about it and attended seminars touting the possibility of it. I understood this as being true: yet experiencing it by continually attempting direct experiences with regard to speaking my future into existence gave me the solidity of knowing that I knew. Where do these experiences come from and how do miracles appear? Here is my assertion; speaking from and into the nothing that surrounds you causes reality and often creates the space for miracles to come into existence.

When you are ready to begin applying this new point of view, please remember the metaphor about the elephant. Given some thought, it will assist you immensely in receiving the value I am placing in front of you. You now know about placing something into the Box. You will have read about proactively, consciously choosing or creating a designated context for this box to have the purpose of having something nonproductive lose its power and significant meaning within your context or space. These actions turn the negative thoughts, meanings and beliefs into nothing, Nothing but a trivia. It all boils down to a simple conscious choice, that of recognizing the power of your own voice and taking back—appropriating--the power within your own voice.

If a person speaks, rather than 'thinks' into the space that is everywhere, is unlimited, increases when used and has only to be recognized and appropriated the results are;

"As a Man Speaks, so it is"

You do have a choice. You create reality with your speaking, or you allow others to create it by listening to them tell you what is real. When you learn to speak with your voice's true authority, your word becomes law in your universe. Want proof? Take a few minutes to think this through. Aren't there about seven billion people on this planet with different realities? How can this thing called reality be a given when seven billion people are claiming to live in seven billion different realities? Sure, there are some similarities like water for drinking, food for eating, yet even those have their twists. Grubs to some people are a delicious treat. Live monkey brains in China are a particular delicacy. Language and beliefs are creative acts that are used consciously or unconsciously, as you choose. This does not happen overnight; it takes training, alertness and practice.

There are places where a border, an imaginary line of agreement drawn in the dirt, result in financial reality that can be as different as night and day, based on one thing: the spoken word and agreement that it is true. Now that is the language of agreement, pure power on display. What happens is that past realities are discussed, reviewed, rehashed, deciphered, thought about, talked about, argued about, debated, held meeting about, gossiped about and mumbled about daily, usually with a complaint about the way it is. Does anything ever change? No, but it is still a creative act, be it unconscious or conscious. It is still the way it is. The word 'about' refers to the past in love with attention and control, causing the recreation of the reality that is, while giving it more power. What follows is that human beings become caught up in what 'they' say is and was so, resulting in the diminishment and the lost memory of their power to transform what is.

Cattle follow the herd. What 'they' say is real to them. Regurgitating what was and is, repeatedly chewing their cud. What would be possible if just one person would create, by speaking a desired reality and said this is what I see? He would be ignoring a given reality, ignoring what others see as real. A crazy person comes to mind for sure, but what if he did not defend his point of view, his truth? What if he simply acquired some agreement and did not make the reality that is present to numerous people wrong? Then could a group of people choose to alter there point of view in agreement, therefore seeing what the first person saw? It is a bit like pretending, making believe, creating, acting as if, assuming, hoping, having faith, praying as if it is already so. What might happen in time? Might, over time, those who have said this is the way it is {the past} start doubting their point of view? I don't know about you, but this is what I see it takes to cause progress. It is proactive, not reactive. The way we attempt to change or fix things that are not the way we want them is massively outdated. This right/wrong game of speaking 'in order to get' or destroy causes nothing but wars and bitterness as it assumes we live in a world of shortage of everything.

Let's use another example to get my point across. When presented with a question that we do not know the answer to, 'I don't know' seems to be a very honest response, based on our past and present reality. When this response is looked at from the point of view of your words having power and is being spoken into your own listening, it actually causes the stifling of the knowledge we strive for.

We think that by telling the truth, things will change. 'I don't know' in some people seems to have the power to create feelings, thoughts and meanings of less than, thoughts and feelings of being stupid or ignorant, feelings of inadequacy, withdrawal from, frustrations, quitting, giving up and so on. Some people have been labeled or have labeled themselves as ignorant based on not knowing certain things, thinking they should know. Well, what if one could alter that reality simply by placing 'I don't know' on a piece of paper and placing it within the Box? Over time the meanings, which empower the words, would slowly loose their power, as these meanings, feelings and thoughts are what block our receiving of knowledge. 'I don't know' would just be 'I don't know' without the meaning and feelings attached to it, opening up the door to knowledge.

When this very popular statement, 'I don't know' is seen as your present reality and is written it on a piece of paper and consciously placed within the Box you designated as a space/context for nothing but a trivia, what might happen? What would be the results of proactively consciously choosing to place 'I don't know' within a designated space where it becomes nothing, Nothing but a trivia? What might happen if the past meanings that caused the feelings begin to drop away? I don't know would have the space to just 'be' allowing knowledge to slowly begin to surface once the past reality of 'I don't know' has lost its power and control of our reality?

You see, life has taught me and continues to teach me that there is nothing to get. What is necessary is to discover and transform the meanings and feelings around the problem that is causing the lack of receiving. This truth, when realized, is that not knowing is actually the gateway to knowledge once the meanings and feelings of the past are transformed. "I don't know,' when discovered as the cause of not knowing allows knowledge the space to be present once again. When 'I don't know' is placed within the Box, over time and practice, meanings, beliefs, thoughts and feelings regarding the past programing of not knowing will begin to diminish.   To say it another way, we live in a world of dualities. In order for knowledge to be present, we must allow not knowing the space to simply 'be' without the thoughts, feelings that meanings and labels cause. Viewing ourselves as context or space allows both I know and I do not know the space to just be. You will eventually experience 'I don't know' loosing its voice and power over you. The same principle applies to 'I don't understand.' Write it in a piece of paper, place it in the Box and it will be transform into nothing, Nothing but a trivia.

You can apply this to writer's block, getting lost, lack of energy, worry, anxiety, over eating, boredom, rejection, lack of time, to much time, almost any habit, confusion, poor memory, bad memories from the past, childhood memories, wrongs done to you, failed business deals, fatigue and more. When self is viewed as a context/space as opposed to a thing, the totality of a human being is accessible. True choice is the reward as the past has lost its power to cause thoughts or speaking.

Example: In your past, which is still in your present, simply notice that you have allowed something--a thought, meaning, belief, circumstance, habit, feeling, perceived reality, way of being, action to enter your space/context. Once this is recognized as being "what is' with meanings attached to it, consciously choose to write 'what is' down on a piece of paper, and place it within the Box. It is a place you have designated for something (the thought, meaning, feeling or belief) to be transformed into nothing, Nothing but a trivia. This will allow it to just 'be' within the context/space of who you are without the past meanings, thoughts and feelings. You have just taken back the lost power of your word. It will simply transform into 'what is'.

At the point where you have deposited your note into the Box, you are choosing to now be at cause, in control or returned to your true self, your power. You have now purposely, consciously "created" a void. You have "created" nothing by speaking it into existence. Please do not diminish the accomplishment of this miracle. Once the transformation is present, your future, where there 'was' something, there will now be space or nothing and the space of nothing is where you can create anew by speaking your future reality.

The new language **you speak** now begins to 'use you' as it now contains the power you unknowingly gave away--the choice to accept or reject the meaning that was attached to the belief, thought or issue. What you have placed in the Box is now in the process of becoming nothing, Nothing but a trivia. When and if the thought or issue surfaces again you can now address it as nothing but a trivia. You are addressing your past with your voice and you now have authority over it regaining power over you. Again, in time and with practice it will soon fade into the distant past. This process when repeated creates this mysterious thing called nothing or the space for something new. Remember the story about my friend placing the issue from his past into the back of his truck and then into the trailer he eventually was able to let it go. Suggesting to him the creation of the trailer and asking him put the past issue into it caused his past to loose its power and control over him.

That experience happened prior to discovering the power of putting something within a context and discovering the amazing power within speaking the word trivia. It resulted in the creation of this Box. I wanted to prove to myself that this process worked by recognizing, appropriating and harnessing the transformational power of a context and the speaking of the word **trivia.**

Chapter Twenty Six

Affirmations and Assertions

Similar, yet the results are different.
Affirmations seldom change anything and require a tremendous amount of work. So what is the problem? What is missing? Why don't they product the results others claim they do? It is as simple as looking up the word in the dictionary or on the net.
The definition of an affirmation is:
1. The act or an instance of affirming; a state of being affirmed,
2. The assertion that something exists or is true.
3. Something that is affirmed. A statement or proposition that is declared to be true.
4. Confirmation or ratification of the truth or validity of a prior judgment, or decision,
5. A solemn declaration accepted instead of a statement under oath.

*** Note: Affirmations are also generally statements of something that is desired, but not true as of the utterance.

Okay, I get that, but here is the rub. Into what are you affirming? Could it be that we are attempting to affirm something into the space of something that is already been assigned a meaning, into the mind that is already occupied with the past beliefs or thoughts? There is a premise stating that; 'No two things can occupy the same space at the same time.' I think you can see the huge effort required for an affirmation to change things or fix them when all thoughts are viewed as powerful things. When we attempt to fix or change the past by using the same power that keeps the past in place, {thoughts) we are attempting to think or read affirmations into ourselves where the past belief or thoughts already are. The well known postulate; 'Nature abhors a void' might come into play here as to an easier, faster way to cause a change. Namely, first create a void for nature or your true self to fill. Creating a void is far more effective than repeating affirmations. It is when one thought is singled out, addressed and 'spoken to' as being nothing but a trivia, that the power of transformation becomes available, within reach. You are 'creating' space, context or nothing.

Now let us look closely at the word assert as it is stated in the dictionary:

"To act, to assert positively from a state of being. To demonstrate. To speak or act in a manner that compels recognition especially of one's rights."

The first part of the definition of assertion is "to act." One of the principal definitions of acting is to pretend. To pretend is to step into another reality. Having to let go or transform the reality you are in is to step into nothing being experienced now. Then we have 'to assert positively,' meaning to behave or speak strongly. To demonstrate.

Again, into what are we asserting or demonstrating? The past that is occupied with something---a thought, meaning, belief, or a way of being. Then we have to speak or act in a manner that compels recognition, especially of one's rights. Even when we speak to ourselves about our rights, we run into the same thing, the past. What is missing here? Might it be the same thing mentioned before, this slippery thing called space or context or nothing?

Makes you wonder doesn't it? I also have wondered, experienced not knowing, letting go, losing control and bingo! A secret truth showed up. If we are attempting to affirm something to ourselves, (speaking or thinking into our own listening) while something within is affirming the opposite, then we are attempting to place something in a space that is already occupied by something called a past belief of thinking we know, something we have evidence of being true.

This is something the mind of our past--in love with attention and control--seems to have power or influence over us. This part of our mind of past usually causes resistance, a stalemate or lack of results. With many hours of daily repeated affirmations and effort we might make some progress. But what if there was a faster, easier way to alter those parts of ourselves that are not optimal to our desired way of being? What could cause a true shift resulting in the changes we desire? What might be the cause of this shift? Could it be our own language spoken to ourselves into the space of nothing? Could we become the same thing as the Box--a context/space where something turns into nothing? Might we also be the cause of what we call something---who we think we are? Could we hold ourselves responsible for unconsciously allowing the language of others to create our context. I assert that we are responsible once we choose to view ourselves as cause. Remember being at cause is choosing to be being responsible for 'what is and what isn't' without all those meanings (bad, wrong, regret, guilt,) attached to those beliefs and thoughts.

There is a very subtle distinction in regard to affirming and assertion. Affirming comes from thinking thoughts; it is an attempt to get something that is missing. The act of assertion speaks, stating that it is true now. If you watch certain politicians they assert, and we affirm. I find this very interesting. Couldn't we just recognize and appropriate the power we gave away and simply start asserting it by speaking up? Could it be as easy as asserting what was true (being at cause and responsible) prior to us giving up the power of our voices of authority? Almost like time travelling through our memory banks and choosing to appropriate, take back to give life back to a part of ourselves we simply forgot was true. To give life back to---to recognize, to appropriate, to give attention to.

If you look deeper you will see what I see. Do affirmations work when asserted? Well, if I assert it to myself over and over and over again, it might stick. What if there is a well kept and guarded secret regarding this thing we call the reality of our past and of our future?

What if it really is just *something* that is impressionable within each of us? And how might it be molding, impressing and arousing our past and future realities? Once becoming aware of this well guarded secret we could become upset and start a war of words (all wars and divorces) and that would get us all fired up with ego. Or we could go live in a closet, blocking out this reality that seems so powerful. But what if there was another way? What if once this something was recognized and appropriated it contained the power and control over your past in love with attention and would produce the results you wanted?

There is this way, and it is located within ever human being. It is a gift we have misused. It, when used with some degree of sanity, magnifies in power, and is unlimited. It increases with use...and it is hidden in plain sight. This gift is acquired by recognition and appropriation. It can be taken, molded, aroused, altered and changed to fit your desires, as it is the precious free gift we have somehow forgotten. We have been conned into believing this gift--our voices—have no power, no authority over the past or the future.

Now comes the best part as I root around in the soil of being conned and discover another sliver of a truth. An assertion must be placed somewhere that has no preconceived notions of reality assigned by another, no designated rules as to what something is to be used for. An assertion must be spoken into a void, into nothing.

What might this sliver of truth be? It is the **Box**. **Something for Nothing.**

Is it hidden from your view? Not now, it is recognized.

Where might it be located? In your space or context.

Who owns this space of the magic of transformation?

You do. You appropriated it. You own the Box. It is the Void, the Nothing, the missing something with no past beliefs, no past thoughts, no history, no perceived value. The Box that contains nothing until you assign it a purpose, a value, agreements, rules, just like a refrigerator, a book, a toilet, a chair, etc.

Wow! I just purchased a Book and a Void or Nothing? Before you throw this book across the room, give me a chance to settle the mind of past in love with attention and control. You unconsciously create voids and fill voids each and every day. As a few examples: You wake up, leave the bed = void created. You go back to bed = filled a void. You pick up a toothbrush = void created. You set it back down = void filled. You leave your residence = void created. You come home, enter your residence = void filled. We move our cars = void created. We drive our cars into voids = filling a void. Each day we are creating voids and filling voids in our wakes. We just don't think about this, as we, like the fish are blind to the value of the 'nothing' that surrounds us.

Your voice of authority over the past can 'choose' to speak and create the purpose of the Box and assign/create its value. It is the space of Nothing {the void} you can utilize and it now will have power over your past. It, the Box now has a silent but powerful voice you created, giving you the values you designated it to be used for, your own transformation. Like the examples of the bed, the toothbrush and the refrigerator, it will cause you to automatically, eventually unconsciously react to the purpose you created. This is you creating a context that uses you, allowing you to receive its value.

Again, your voice of authority. It has to be recognized and appropriated. Your voice is free because you already have it. There is nothing you have to get. What might come against you using your voice of authority by placing something into this space, this Box, this void? Resistance? I agree. Resistance coming from where?

Might it be a notion, belief or thought from the past doing the resisting, asserting itself saying something like; 'they' say the past can NOT be changed? Now, what if resistance lost its power over you? What if 'they'--the collective unconscious--say resistance is something you must control, overcome by force or something you must learn to let go of. 'They' did say that and still do. So, now we are clear that following what 'they' say is being a victim of the voice I talk about here and in an earlier book I wrote, "Victims of the Voice". How might one get a handle on that voice, that voice which is doing the resisting?

First we must recognize the thoughts or voice as coming from the past, in love with attention and control. Then recognize the past as being the cause of the thoughts; the meanings attached to resistance. Then place resistance in the Box you assigned for the purpose of turning the meanings into nothing-- Nothing but a trivia. What will be left is a ten letter word with no power over you. Remember 'resistance' is now just 'what is', minus its meanings. Once it becomes a trivia, couldn't you continue to choose to give it a meaning, a silly name, response with laughter when resistance presents itself, being as it is nothing, Nothing but a trivia?

What might happen over time to that conversation, the one you unconsciously allowed to be inserted into your space or context called, 'Resistance is something and it is powerful' and has become a powerful belief. Once placed within the Box it will be transformed, stripped of its meanings and it will loose its power and control over you. Who or what might show up? You with the power of your own voice of authority now speaking into the Box, a space void of the meanings attached to resistance.

Ooops, I forgot to tell you where this 'space or nothing' is located --- Everywhere!

Every living, breathing breath we breathe is the space to create our reality without having to fight or deal with resistance. Resistance within your space/context is an illusion. It is nothing but a trivia, if and when you say it is so. Usually it is the 'they said', the collective unconscious, that creates the resistance being present, but in reality there is no resistance. There are rules in place that create resistance, yet they are all made up into societies and nature's agreements. Resistance itself can be used and is being used, once recognized and appropriated. An example of this could be a surfer. He uses resistance to give him the thrill of the ride. He is on top of it, becoming the source of his joy as he uses its power, the resistance beneath his board.

"Any man who reads too much and uses his own brain too little falls into lazy habits of thinking." © Albert Einstein

Chapter Twenty Seven

Fear or Mental Chatter

This thing I call the mental *chatter or the committee of our minds* of the past is everywhere, permeating our very existence. It runs amuck, causing havoc in everything it touches. Like a silent plague it sneaks into the cracks of sanity and common sense, eroding even the very fabric of personal responsibility. The practice of valuing one's own word and honoring that power has been silently slipped into the deck of priorities--lost in the shuffle of dealing with the numerous issues of life. Jokers have usurped the place of recognition, shifting our attention to their antics--their shenanigans. Shock and awe, lies, cons, injustices, personal attacks, lawsuits, diseases, statistics, secrets systems, violence, and dramas are flooded into our consciousness, and are gaining ground. Each of these repetitive insertions into our consciousness has the potential of causing thoughts of fear and powerlessness. Seeing no way to stop or escape the onslaught, we slide into the safety of oblivion, into the state of barely functioning, semiconscious and even further into a state of non-think.

As I recalled the process of discovering the cause of anxiety I had long ago experienced I became privy to another interesting unit of mental chatter dangling in a corner crack of my own space/context. I was not only afraid, I was afraid of fear itself.

In 1933, seven years prior to my birth, Franklin D. Roosevelt addressed the Nation at the depth of a depression stating that, "The only thing we have to fear is fear itself." This statement, which he asserted as the truth, still governs our country as of this writing.

Fearing this something labeled fear, as stated by FDR in 1933, has had tremendous and significant meanings attached to it for some 82 years and is now being used, among other things, and by other people to force other nations and people into submission. This fear, this collective unconscious is used daily to con us out of our money, our resources, out of our homes and rob us of our rights. Confusion is its soul mate.

But what if this belief, this emotion called fear is just an illusion? Something invented that seeks power and control over us? Could it possibly be coming from the mind of our past that creates this fear that is generated from a belief? Why? Answer, to stay in power and hold us within its control and keep us from discovering the untapped potential within ourselves. The past along with the collective unconscious needs our agreement to remain in power and control.

There is an opposing principle that addresses this issue of fear: Job 3:25 states; "For the thing which I greatly feared is come upon me, and that which I was afraid of is come unto me."

When I took the time to decisively study this subject, I came up again and again noticing something hidden in plain sight. If we, at birth, are thrown into conversations or beliefs of fearing fear itself, fear must be a something, do you agree? Where is this conversation located? Within our context, our space.

Now, what if this thing called fear was placed within the Box? Might it too go poof, and with out the meanings from the past transform into nothing but a trivia, becoming powerless? Use common sense: without certain fears, who would we be? Indeed, who would we be?

Let's step into the future and take a look at who or what this might produce. Fear has been placed in the box and transformed into a trivia as opposed to something big and powerful. Let's use-taking action as an example as fear is usually what has stopped us from taking action in the past. I, now being privy to the knowledge and experience of fear being nothing but a trivia, would be aware of my mind's mental chatter as it encountered other thoughts of action that were still stuck in the illusion of fear as being powerful. A past thought of action would appear expecting to encounter fear, yet fear is now a trivia. What caused this fearful expectation from taking action? The past illusion of fear being powerful. I could use this knowledge to frighten those thoughts of taking action simply with my presence, my voice—if I wanted to as I now have a choice. I am in control of fear being powerful or being a trivia. The mind of past in love with attention and control would begin to feel the loss of power and control as the mind of past would feel threatened. It would want to defend its position.

Rather than arguing, fighting, resisting, debating, out maneuvering, making it wrong, overpowering, denying its presence, threatening or trying to fix or change it. What if I recognized and simply acknowledged the past thought of the fear of taking action having power and control over me? (Briefly gave it the attention and control it is in love with). Being as I now have a choice, couldn't I simply thank the mind of past for all its tedious work, efforts and struggles over the years in keeping me safe. Appreciating its help in arriving at this place in time and I tell it that I will take over for now. What might happen here? Might this mind in love with attention mellow out; take a chill pill, having just received exactly what it has been searching for? The answer is yes and this has to be 'experienced' to know that you know.

Using my voice of authority over the mind of past by asserting and causing (speaking) the thoughts of fear to be nothing but a trivia, soothed and eventually silenced the thoughts of fear being something to be afraid of. It became a feeling, nothing more, no chatter. In this example I am the one acknowledging, giving attention to the mind of past that is in love with attention. Remember this mind of past is with your context, you have it, not 'it' has you. I am recognizing it. I am bigger. This is what causes the mind of the past to quiet down, allowing my true self to appear. Arguing, maneuvering, starving, fighting against, overpowering, tricking, out changing or attempting to fix this mind of past in love with attention is futile.

Creating a working relationship with the mind of past works wonders. Speaking language or beliefs to my mind of past and asserting my spoken thoughts and meanings as new facts allows me to be in control of my life.

I am on to something here. This is what the mind of past was up against. It is now somewhat afraid of me, as it is now in a secondary position. I am on to its game.

I am now aware of the game of divide and conquer being played out by the mind of past. It is the same game a pickpocket uses to lift someone's wallet. The game is this; the mind of past, once in power, attempted to use the power of its thoughts, feelings and beliefs against me. As it inserted those diversions into my limited attention span, which in the past I allowed it to use me through out the day, it caused my attention to be diverted to the very fear thoughts and feelings I was afraid of. Pocket number one successfully picked. I did not get what I was after.

Up pops another small amount of negative conversation or a twinge of fear and I complain, becoming again a victim of its voice, stating that this in not fair, not right. My limited attention span is again diverted to another matter, another fearful thought and pocket number two is picked. I was waiting for the action that will cause the fear in me to call me to action--but then just maybe I was still afraid of the fear itself as FDR stated.

I now know it is simply the illusion of fear the mind of past in love with attention created from its need of attention and control. It then makes grand proclamations of it power to create something new in the future and then takes action against me by not delivering on its promises. Pocket number three is picked.

Change, to the mind of past running unchecked or uncontrolled, threatens its power, its control. Even the thoughts of change can cause it to assert the belief, the illusion of change being scary and unwanted. When change starts to become fun or easy, up pops the fearful feelings, as the mind of past wants me to thinks it is who I am. Each time I allow the mind of past to pick my pocket it robs me of another valuable aspect of who I really am.

Fear = False Evidence Appearing Real. We were taught how to feel 'in order to' fit into the reality created prior to us arriving at birth. No one was allowing or supporting us in choosing to laugh at fear, seeing the illusion it really was, and we slowly forgot we were born with the power to choose meanings for ourselves. Once fear was instilled in us as being powerful, over time we began to question this in the attempt to break free of the conversations of the past, the already given meanings. We found no one agreed with us, so we figure it must be the only reality available. Now we are on automatic, as the conversations are already programmed into us. So much for original thought. Now we get to relive our parents and their parents programmed meanings and feelings. Gee, now that all these illusions are churning around inside our bodies and we, being humans that think, label and create meanings for the feelings we feel, label them as many of the emotional diseases man has invented. A person who is full of energy is drugged down 'in order to' fit into this molded reality created by agreement. We need people to fit in, so we take away their power and program them to just go along and not rock the sinking boat we are all on.

Fear is said to be that feeling of fight or flight that causes us to react. So, we think if no fear, it means no action needed, right? Wrong. It is like someone is waiting to say; "The emperor has no clothes." We all see his naked body, yet who will state it as a fact and cause the action? Here is what I see happening. Slowly, ever so slowly, past thoughts cause feelings to encroach. The past thoughts, being baffling and cunning, attempt to convince us that they are in control and will keep us safe, therefore no action. Could this again be us being afraid of fear itself? Being as no action is triggered the blood of common sense is secretly drained from our consciousness, slowly robbing us of the ability to think for ourselves. Now we are down a pint, slowed down by the bombardment of more outrageous thoughts. Does fear surface alerting us to take action? Not yet. The subtle slow erosion continues to take its toll. Taping into an experience from the past, a continuous dripping of a lackadaisical memory, leak's moment to moment back into our consciousness. We are again creeping toward the predicted future of failure and regret.

We wait and watch for the call to action. But wait, we are susceptible to the lack of action others simulate. What are we waiting for? When is it enough? What does enough look like? Is enough located somewhere outside of ourselves? Might it be located within our voices instead of our feelings? Might we choose to speak enough into existence to ourselves, into our own listening? Might this cause us to take action on what we see, using common sense to invoke and cause speaking? Might this action motivate us to think for ourselves? Are we people of action or reaction? Are we waiting for the feelings of fear to react?

What might happen if we took it upon ourselves to create out of nothing by speaking, asserting that fear had no meaning, no power over us? Stating, asserting, affirming that enough is enough right now. We see it; we know it and we understand it, yet still no action is taken. Each of us 'asserting' the one statement of: 'Enough is enough right now', with the authority within our voices, would soon cause our minds of past in love with attention and control to doubt its own illusionary power and control.

"The meaning I picked, the one that changed my life: Overcome fear, behold wonder." © Richard Bach

As in my assertions of our voices being more powerful than our thoughts, (speaking causing thinking) there is a comparison to be looked at here. Who has the power? It only takes creating new meanings, speaking up with our own voices of power within to cause our once given power to return to its rightful place. (Recognizing and Appropriating). I see no other way to stop this affront from taking us to a place we do not want to go. I have been doing this for sometime and I am doing it as I write. Might we wake up to the fact that we have been conned, bamboozled, hornswoggled, flimflammed, deceived and confused into believing we are powerless statistics or labels instead of contexts or spaces with the power to transform. Assertions of 'they' say continue to gain agreement, power and control, like rumors asserting a supposed fact, creating the realities we experience over time.

What is to stop us from doing exactly what 'they' or our minds of past do? Give attention to (recognize) and take back (appropriate) the power and control over our own lives. Would asserted language spoken as truth create our reality? Could we usurp 'they' and the mind of past in love with attention. Could we recognized and appropriate the power and control we unconsciously gave away? Could we choose to laugh at what 'they' and the mind of past says, viewing both as trivia? Would this action cause a shift in our way of being, would this transform us?

If we choose to look up to the others as our example of how to be, think and act, we come away with being powerless over thoughts, feelings, beliefs, meanings, issues, outside influences and all. Victims of others voices. Don't we want a leader to be at cause, not at the effect. Action, not reaction. Powerful, not powerless. Competent, not incompetent. Victorious not Victim. Responsible, not irresponsible. This is not rocket science. This was taught in kindergarten and in church. So, isn't there is another saying that goes something like this? Be the change you want to see and experience.

"You are always free to change your mind and choose a different future, or a different past." © Richard Bach

Chapter Twenty Eight

Change, Identity Crisis vs. Shift

What is this thing we call an Identity Crisis? What is this thing called a Shift?

Identity: A definition of identity resides in who you are, the way you think and speak about yourself, the way you are viewed by the world and the characteristics that define you.

Crisis: A definition of crisis is that of a crucial or decisive point or situation. Especially a difficult or unstable situation involving an impending change.

Shift: To cause something or someone to move or change from one position or direction to another, especially slightly. The wind is expected to shift to the West tomorrow. Changing of an idea, opinion or point of view.

Change seems to be the operative condition behind these phenomena. Why do we resist this normal part of life when everything in the world is in constant change? Could it be based on past beliefs which have meanings attached to the word change? That change is bad, difficult, fearful, something to be resisted, something we have to fight? Doesn't viewing change in this way turn it into a crisis? Might we put this word 'change' into the Box and transform it into a shift instead of a crisis? Into nothing but a **trivia?**

Expecting something in our future to be better and yet still hoping that we won't have to let go of what we believe, think or speak? Viewing change as simply a shift in beliefs or meanings both creates and allows who we really are to surface, and enables us to allow this change to materialize without all the pain, struggle, frustration and fear.

Shifting is something we do ever day without conscious effort. It is done with ease, welcomed as something good, lacking in fear, danger or frustration. We shift our weight on our feet. If you are like most of us you have been patiently waiting on the shore for an imaginary boat whose desired destination is an island of understanding where issues you now deal with are settled once and for all. A place where those issues have been transformed into the nothingness they are. This island might be called the island of serenity, of self-actualization or peace of mind where we shift our conversations, our ideas, intentions, desires, wants, preferences, and our points of view among other things.

In some way, it is almost as though we are expecting to evolve, to learn something new, yet all the while we are desperately clutching onto our past beliefs. Isn't hanging onto the belief of fearing change setting oneself up for an identity crisis, the very cause of that fear?

Change just is, so why not embrace it with gusto and skip the frustration and the pain of resistance? Would it be possible to alter the meaning we've given to the experience of change, to experience change as being fun, even exciting and welcomed therefore shifting it to an attitude of acceptance? Into the Box it goes. What about even transforming the meanings attached to 'letting go'? We don't like to let go, so why suffer? Letting go could be transformed into a simple shift, not a crisis. Might the unwanted meanings of the pain of letting go disappear? I say it is possible, and it is the optimal way to shift your identity.

To receive the real value of these words, these ideas, a change, shift or transformation must take place. This change will give you great rewards once you allow these new thoughts and ideas to enter your mind and begin to entertain you. You can choose to go willingly or resist it; it is totally up to you. However, if you choose not to go, you will not get the value offered, and be left with the familiar feelings of being conned, leaving you with again the arrogance of being right.

If you are like most of us you have been patiently waiting on the shore for an imaginary boat whose desired destination is an island of understanding where issues you now deal with are settled once and for all. A place where those issues have been transformed into the nothingness they are. This island might be called the island of serenity, of self-actualization or peace of mind.

Many of us expect to be magically transported to the island of serenity, never expecting to at least be required to get on the boat and take the trip. We think like we are taught to think, believe what we were told to believe and act like we were told to act. To be invited onto this island of serenity we must be willing to let go of understanding and step into the unknown of direct experiences.

When at last invited and welcomed onto the boat, we all expect to be accepted as we are. Then we discover that there is but one requirement, and that is to leave one of our most cherished points of view on the shore of past, so as to not sink the boat on the way to the island of your choice.

Tough choice, I agree, but it is that simple. What is this issue we are required to leave on the shore of past, you might ask? Consider letting go of the cherished position of always being right.

You can't continue to unconsciously passionately clutch onto the point of view of being right, thinking you know something you do not know. To arrive on the Island of your choosing you must choose to leave being right on the shore of your past. You must consciously choose to shift your position or point of view, and to be open to possibilities.

Once you have taken the trip, and arrived at your island, you will experience a positional paradigm shift and know through direct experience the costs of being right and thinking you knew what you did not know. You will then be able to recognize when you are again stuck on the position of being right as you will see yourself in others you encounter, knowing the costs to them clutching onto being right. These costs include among others; separation, loss of love, breaks in belonging, anger, frustration, pain, disease, confusion, lack of worth, feeling trapped within the subjugated box, stress, helplessness, being at the effect of others language, grave losses, loneliness, dramas, lack of power and lack of control.

As far as taking up residence there, well there are an abundance of cottages available and they are rent-free. The choice will now be yours.

These encounters with others will become gifts, as they will present to you a reminder of the choice to shift again, to give up the position of being right, as you now know its costs. You will have based on something much more valuable than understanding: direct experience. You will be on that island without the issues, thoughts, meanings and beliefs of the past running your life and you will know that you know how you got there. Rightness will transform into ease, clarity and correctness. Lack of power will be transformed into personal power, lack of control over your mind of past will be a distant memory. Being effected by others will bounce off you, friendships will be numerous, anger will be transformed into being at ease, loneliness will be replaced with delighting in your own company. Lack of self-worth will dissolve, returning you to yourself. Frustrations will shift into acceptances, and the feelings of being trapped within the box of subjugation will be replaced with the freedom you experiences as a child.

"Self-reverence, self-knowledge, self-control; these three alone lead one to sovereign power." © Alfred Lord Tennyson

Chapter Twenty Nine

Experiencing Language

The author of Recovery International, Dr. Abraham Low, states that the time of past can be overcome by the repetitive training of the mind. That training comes from you choosing to speak to your mind of past from a new point of view. A point of view of you having power and authority over it. It can and is intended to be directed, as it is a gift with its true purpose being that of serving you and your purposes. It is intended to work for you, not you being a slave to it. You have allowed, by not choosing to think for yourself, the creature comforts of unconscious choices to enter and do their biding, robbing you of your true self. You allowed your mind of past to have you, as opposed to you having your mind of choice. Thoughts thought you, as opposed to you thinking your own thoughts.

Once the mind of your past is addressed as what it is, your power, your authority and your voice will replace the powerlessness and confusion. Being off center or unbalanced will be replaced by being centered and balanced, and a lack of focus will be overridden by clear powerful focus. You will now know where you are going, and you will have the knowledge and tools you have acquired by direct experiences. You will know how to get where you choose to go.

You will also feel the shift that has taken place within yourself when you encounter the rightness in others, and recognize it as the choice you made to give it up. Observing the wrongness in others will also be another clue or reminder of your choice to give up the position of being right. Where wrongness is present, rightness still lurks within. It is the mindset of the past attempting to insert its intention; that of having power, of being in control. This right--wrong interaction is actually a game of the mind as it attempts to keep secret the potential value each person is attempting to add to your life. It is a form of separation, divide and conquer, keeping you unaware of your true identity and potential.

*** I am now going on a walkabout. Enjoy! ***

It was during the time I was reading Jonathan Livingston Seagull by Richard Bach that I first experienced words coming to life. Becoming totally enthralled by his prose caused creatures to appear to me each with their unique personalities. As I continued to read I found myself caught up, consumed, usurped within his story as living images feverishly bid for my attention. Over time I found myself literally lost inside the book, having let go of the reality that surrounding me. As I continued to read, I would often stop to look around for a few moments as I sensed time running at a speed governed by these new thoughts. Each time I would take a moment to pause, my world spontaneously morphed into a unseen reality as each new thought fought for life, attempting to overwhelm some of the ones that had been previously planted in my mind.

A battle had begun to stir within and without; limiting thoughts, undeniable truths, realities others believed in, don't limit the is, sacrifice boredom, listen to your selfishness, practice being fictional, argue your limitations and sure enough they're yours, and problems have gifts. These ideas randomly plummeted into my space as these new thoughts fought to grab a hold of me, each pleading desperately to be given a chance at living. I thought; could this book be allowing me to view possibilities never considered before?

Seagull are fairly common in San Diego, mostly along our beaches, yet after reading this book, seagulls seemed to appear almost randomly, and ostensibly from out of nowhere. I live about 15 miles inland, so seeing a seagull is not a daily event, but each time they would appear I would be transported back to parts of the story of Jonathan. It was something I could relate to. Being a recent divorcee was still fresh within my new reality, and I felt at times an outcast myself. Just knowing that someone seemed to have felt this pain before, even if it was only a seagull, kept me from crashing during those 300 mile-per-hour dives of emotion. I too was beginning to discover myself, my mistakes and I was teachable. My mind opened and I let it in. This possibility, that if I practiced I could fly, learning to ride the high winds, dining on the delicate insects located in the ether of thought ignited within me a fire that began to burn, setting aflame desire, the desire to experience.

Now free flying like a bird is not something we humans have mastered yet, but the way I heard what was possible took on many meanings in the future. I heard flying as the possibility of there being an open door to freedom from the pain I was in. Little tidbits of Bach's book would show up now and then as I began the adventure of self- discovery somewhat late in life. I have written about some of those experiences in prior books, yet where I am now, writing this book is beyond even my wildest dreams and wishes. I wished to be given the talent, to be guided into experiencing the writing of a book that had the potential of making a huge difference in adding value to others lives.

Some time later the book "Illusions" appeared in my life as a gift from one of my daughters, also written by Richard Bach. When I read his books something touched a part of me that had been in complete atrophy for the length of my then 37 years. He demonstrated this something in the story about Jonathan Livingston Seagull, yet it was not until I opened his book Illusions that it stirred a restless part of me pleading for recognition. He began his book with pages covered in grease and I experienced his brilliance. I did not understand it I experienced it. There is a huge distinction between understanding and experiencing, and I was beginning to discover their gifts.

"Reality is merely an illusion, albeit a very persistent one."
© Albert Einstein

As I have viewed life, we humans have an insatiable appetite for information. Answers are sought after as they were in the gold rush of the 1900's. Thoughts such as: if only I knew this or that, then my life would be better. And if only I had this or that, then I would be happy. Or, why do bad things happen to good people? Then there is: why do the bad people get away with things? These ideas constantly permeate our consciousness. I too was on this treadmill, seeking answers to my questions. Seeking answers--how to make life fit into my thoughts and beliefs. Many sleepless nights followed, along with the pain of not understanding.

As I mentioned earlier I once heard the saying, "Understanding is the bobby prize." This was a statement made by Werner Erhard, the founder of est in the late 70's. Now, I did hear it as it was spoken and I thought I understood it, but it hit me as a, "so what?" kind of statement. I still needed to understand, and it was not until many years later that the full power of that statement caught up with me as I was still chasing understanding. Somehow the value of experience was able to overpower my rightness and take hold of my ever-pursuant nature.

In the book "Illusions" there is a quote; "Your only obligation in any lifetime is to be true to yourself. Being true to anyone else or anything else is not only impossible, but the mark of a fake messiah." At the time I read that quote I was on a road traveled by many. I did not have a clue about discovering who I was, let alone what I was capable of.

Once I admitted I was responsible for having been true to everyone except myself, I discovered that I was unconsciously controlled by thoughts and desires that were not my own. I then began to peel away the layers of what I had allowed to enter my world. The demands of more speed and the illusion of perfection permeated my psyche. My core beliefs caused me to rebel against being overdrawn into bankrupting my allotment of personal time and energy. I had to choose. I had to think for myself. I had to find my own voice.

The steps between thinking I knew who I was, and beginning to discover my own truth was filled with pitfalls and the pain of not understanding myself, my world—anything. Being thwarted from being my true self in the early years of my life had now driven me on to look within, learning to transform the experiences of sheer terror and apprehension into the ease in which water gently trickles down a stream. I can now watch a leaf float effortlessly down a stream and in certain moments I can connect with it, knowing we are one.

Looking back, it was worth it all. Coming out the other side was filled with the true joy of knowing who I was, knowing how to experience life, and not just live it.

"Mastering others is strength. Mastering yourself is true power." © Lao Tzu

Chapter Thirty
Something into Nothing
Nothing into Something

On a more personal note. Being as you have come this far, being patient enough to allow me to share my views and discoveries about viewing oneself and others as context/space, you might see this as a possible way of being in life. Without labels and meanings of good or bad, right or wrong, lacking the imposed statistics of being a thing, you soon will have a choice to make. You might choose to apply these principles or discoveries to your own life, by creating and viewing yourself as a context. It would be like going back to the beginning and recognizing and appropriating the *something* you unknowingly gave away. Maybe a second chance at consciously choosing what to believe, what to think, how to act, and how to be. In this way of being nothing/space/context, couldn't you then create yourself as you did when you were a child? Freed from the subjugated box, free to pretend and make believe; being free to discover and free to be anything or anyone?

So, you might ask with a twinge of angst, "how does this fit into my life as an adult, this game of make believe?" The soft answer goes something like this: You are asleep. You must wake up. The toughest answer to hear is that you are still making up your life as we speak. You just forgot that we all have the ability and the power to govern our lives.

The sad part to hear is that once grasped, once recalled, once remember and accepted as a fact, we arrive at the realization that we have been conned. It is as though we are all still run by a voice that says, children are to be seen and not heard. We are also stuck in a game we played called Hide and Seek, and some of us forgot to come home. Someone called 'olly olly oxen free!' but we did not hear it. Now we think this game is the only game we are allowed to play, and as of now it is permeating our lives, showing up in the divorce rates, discourse among people, and in the breaking down of the family unit.

This may seem to be horrible news to hear, but there is a huge upside reward once this is heard and accepted. It is not to late to choose to utilize the authority, the power of your voice to direct your mind and have your thoughts do your biding. You now have within you a voice of your own authority, and it still has the power to assert itself once you allow it to step forth. You can still cause and create, making up a completely new shift in your way of being in your life. You just forgot to do it consciously. It takes practice and patience both with yourself and others, but it is still possible.

There are many moments in our lives that trigger these memories of our past. Each one is a choice to stay true to ourselves or quietly slip into the safety of hiding. To go home is mirrored in the movie ET, directed by Steven Spielberg. We feel a break in our connection with self, of belonging, and the urge is to go home. We still hear the call of safety, the feeling of freedom, but in the search to connect we enter confusion and doubt as to where home is located. Attempting to understand that safety and freedom are always 'within' thwarts the minds ability to process 'within', triggering us being afraid of the illusion of fear. This cannot be done with the mind of past in love with attention and control. It must be done by who you really are, choosing to consciously, proactively step into the unknown of nothing. In that single moment in time you are out of your mind. Not crazy as some might think, but on your way home to the safety and freedom you unknowingly gave away. I like to call it coming out of the closet, the closet of hiding who you really are.

You are now in present time, standing alone, and at first unbalanced, yet alive.

Think back to the last miracle you witnessed. Where did it come from? Unexplainably, something turned into nothing or nothing turned into something. That is all there is. The example above is about the choice of stepping from being the some 'thing' created by labels, beliefs and the language of thoughts put upon us when we were unconscious, to choosing to step into nothing, and standing on nothing, being supported by the newly remembered authority of your word. We did this when we were children, we made it up, we invented and we created everything--from nothing. We gave ourselves permission and we gave ourselves agreement.

So, how does one tap into this ability to shift their way of being? As I stated, there is a premise, which asserts that two things cannot occupy the same space at the same time. Now what? What if? What if we could create our being nothing from something? We could place ourselves inside the Box, yet trust me there is an easier way. We have been labeled or we labeled ourselves. We have allowed others the place thoughts, meanings, beliefs and feelings into our contexts and become statistics or 'some thing'. The same principle that applies to the Box, applies to us. Once we transform our labels, thoughts, beliefs, meanings and feelings into trivias, we are transformed into nothing. Nothing meaning the empty space of a new unassigned, not yet asserted context.

"Not being known doesn't stop the truth from being true."
© Richard Bach

As explained earlier, we also were created into something from nothing. We were conceived. From nothing we became something. When you come to the realization that you have labeled yourself or allowed others to label you as 'some thing' you can now choose to transform the labels and meanings into trivia by placing them within the Box. Without the labels and meanings you are at true choice, therefore context. This is who you are, nothing or no thing.

For example, if 'I am a worrier' is in your space/context

and you placed it in the Box to be turned into nothing but a trivia, you could now invent, create, speak, make up a conversation called, "I no longer worry'. Write it down on a piece of paper and put (using your language, your voice of authority) 'I am a worrier' into the context or space of 'something for nothing' (the Box). Over time, with practice and repetition 'I am a worrier' will be transformed into nothing but a trivia as it will lose its meanings. Remember you assigned the purpose of this Box or context. You will now have created a void where 'I no longer worry' will replace your past conversation and become your new reality. At first you might hear the mind of past in love with attention expressing its chatter of control of your language, even telling you that you are lying to yourself. Simply recognize it and say 'thank you for sharing' (giving it a bit of your attention) and continue on. We all know rejection is tough to deal with, so be gentle but firm when you address the mind that is in love with attention and power.

Once this is experienced, miracles then become possible as you are speaking into a space you designated the agreements to be called: Something for Nothing; something transforming into a trivia. Something with no resistance attached to it. It just is, no meaning.

There are three steps in this process. as I will again clarify:

Step One: Recognize what is present in your space/context that is undesirable. (Example, worry).

Step Two: Write it down on a piece of paper, fold it up, and place it in the Box, while speaking it out loud in the beginning--having authority over the circumstance, issue, meaning, thought or belief, telling it; (worry) that it is Nothing, nothing but **a trivia**.

Step Three: Create your language based upon what was missing as an assertion of what is present now: "I am finally free from worry." As you speak this as who you are now, the language you have created will eventually cause you to feel its presence in your **future**. As the feeling becomes stronger, you will feel the shift. This is the evidence of the new language using you, just like the old language used you. You are now creating your life from the future, not you past. Should any past thoughts or beliefs come up, place them in the Box. Remember the story about the stick person within the context. You are bigger than what you are asserting as being a trivia. Reflect: Rome was not build in a day. Be patient. Remember the elephant story.

In the beginning it takes a bit of courage to allow yourself this stepping out to materialize into this space--time--reality. It takes dropping your act and yes; we all have our act of powerlessness over issues, meanings, things, beliefs, thoughts and circumstances. This is just a simple shift in your point of view of who you thought you were in the past. Shifting, like the choices we made to become Cowboy or Indian or Mother or Child when we were playing make believe some years ago. Once a few shifts are experienced, like shifting from worrier to not worrying, this becomes a successful memory you can draw on, knowing it is possible as it is based on your direct experience. You now know that you know.

Now the future attempts will become less threatening and a whole lot easier. Over time and practice, placing things in the **Box** like stress, worry, sleeplessness, confusion, boredom, perfectionism, the workaholic, shopaholic, shortage of time, forgetfulness, low energy, fatigue, lack of focus and more come to be seen as possibilities you can overcome as they can also be transformed from something into nothing, Nothing but a trivia.

"One creates from nothing. If you try to create from something you're just changing something. So in order to create something you first have to be able to create nothing." © Werner Erhard

Chapter Thirty One

Applying my Discovery

Throughout my quest, in search of the something that would rid me of the anxiety, my focus and energy had been severely depleted, yet language continued to be presented as the mysterious key that could reveal to me the something I did not know I did not know.

Looking back, I remember the moment I discovered the power in this unassuming little word trivia through my studies of Recovery International. While looking up its meaning I remembered the premise of James Allen's book, that of 'thought' being the ultimate means in gaining power and control of one's life. I began to wonder. Just maybe this word could be utilized in junction with the something I had discovered. As I recognized and simply appropriated the word trivia, joining it with my speaking, its power surfaced to be experienced, becoming stronger. I then began to experiment with it by applying it on an issue within my context.

I applied it first to the anxiety I thought had been causing me the stress. As I spoke to it as being a trivia the anxiety began to slightly dissipate. I was a bit surprised by its power, the simplicity and the ease of its use. Then I spoke to the stress as being a trivia, and I felt it lighten in its intensity. Caught up in this discovery I stayed with the experiment. Without the anxiety and the stress overriding and overpowering my mental focus I looked again within my context. I remembered and could hear the voices, the past meanings attached to anxiety and stress. Looking again, this time with confidence, I addressed the meanings as trivia. A moment of calmness then filled my body. The discovery was instant. I realized the core cause as being the meanings attached to the words.

I then applied this discovery to the thoughts and meanings that caused the feelings of my depleted lack of energy, now speaking to the meanings as also being **trivia**. Amazingly the meanings left, allowing my energy to return. It was then that I realized that the something I had been searching for was the power located within my voice. I was speaking into a precious present, the presence of now, into the space of nothing.

It was then that I created the Box to represent a place to put Something and transform it into for Nothing.

The magic in these shifts is this. Once you have 'experienced' a few of these shifts, you will know that it is possible based on your own direct experience. Using an example of the game of pretending, let us use, "I have no motivation." That is what is in your space/context as of now. It is what you are experiencing now. The statement, 'I have no motivation,' contains thoughts, beliefs, meanings and feelings that are caused by those words thinking you. They are coming from the past language you unconsciously allowed into your space or context prior to you consciously choosing. The lack of motivation--just words and letters with meanings you've attached to them cause even more thoughts and feelings to appear. You may think it means you are bad, wrong and terrible, even having thoughts of life not being fair. These are thoughts and feelings are something you do not want to be in your space/context anymore. You absolutely know that without motivation you are destined to fail, so you try to find or get motivation. You beg, you hope, you plea, you pray and you wait patiently, sometimes for a lifetime, hoping the right type of motivation will show up. This is what happens, this is what we have been taught to believe. In time motivation may show up, but it is random and unpredictable.

Here is a faster, easier way. You write the belief, the one you believe is true based on your present evidence on a piece of paper, e.g., I have no motivation. You fold it up and insert it into the **Box** that you have consciously, proactively designated to be used for the purpose of turning something into nothing, Nothing but a trivia. You now choose to assert, to speak into the space or void you created, allowing what you have placed into the **Box** to be transformed. 'Having no motivation', this idea is now being transformed into nothing but a trivia--and now has no power over you as it has no meaning. You are bigger. You have spoken, and having authority over it, you now have more power than the thoughts, beliefs, feelings and the meanings that were placed in that Box. You can now face up to the chatter, this mind in love with attention and control, recognize it and acknowledge the mind for sharing its past beliefs. "Thank you for sharing."

The words, delivered in a respectful way, 'Thank you for sharing' is a great way to respond to the mind of past, but remember, do not make the mind of your past wrong. Respect its input, remembering it is just a trivia, and you simply choose to take your control back. You are giving the mind of the past what it needs, (attention) therefore it will quiet down. What you have created is a working relationship with the mind of the past where you now speak to it from the position of authority as opposed to it running your life. If what you placed inside within attempts to come out of the Box, remind it, label it by addressing it as nothing, Nothing but a trivia, telling it to go back to where you put it. Repetition works! Use your newly discovered voice of calm authority. Do not fight, or be on a position of being right with it, just acknowledge it.

Putting something in this **Box** is a proactive act. It's an assertion of something having this meaning or that. In the past, 'nothing' turned into 'something' by receiving agreement and meaning (a bed, a refrigerator, a toothbrush). When 'something' is placed back into nothing, into the Box, there is a new agreement or meaning --- trivia, and poof! Void created. In time that 'something' you declared shows up! Now, I don't know about you, but that was not what I was taught in school. I never read that in the newspapers and I surely did not see that on the boob tube. Can you even take a moment to grasp the possibilities in life that would open up if you could speak and materialize in this way? Far out? Time will tell.

"If you keep saying it the way it really is, eventually your word is law in the universe." © Werner Erhard

Chapter Thirty Two

This Thing called Belief

Asserting one's self, as far as I can tell, truly shapes realities. It is also a power that is being used against us daily as we slowly sink into the dark hole of non-think. I was once privy to directly experiencing an unbelievable spoken reality; 'human beings will believe anything' when I took part in the est training some many years ago. I was caught up in a demonstration of creating reality presented to me during the training and I bought it hook, line and sinker. I considered myself to be fairly intelligent person, though it made absolutely no difference. The story presented to me took me over as easily as snow covers the ground during a winter storm. Luckily for me and about 80 other participants, the experiment was revealed to us as a secret bit of wisdom seldom shared with the collective unconscious. This asserting came from intensely skilled seminar leaders intending to wake us up to the facts of life--that of coming to the realization that we were essentially brainless machines being fed information, robbing us of our true selves. Out of that experience we came to realization that we all still possessed the power to transform our own lives at each and every moment.

This experience began on the third day of the training, shortly before we were about to break for dinner. We had been subjected to many long hours of training and hours of complicated information, along with the many questions that were raised during the exchanges with those who participated with the trainer. This information was referred to as data and it was being intensely discussed in specific detail along with explanations and diagrams of various solutions drawn on blackboards. This experience was similar to brainwashing only with the hope of a positive purpose. You see we paid for this training. As the trainers attempted to pass along this information to us we became physically worn down and mentally our brains had been stretched beyond their normal capacity. Still sitting in our chairs, listening to more data was taking a huge toll on all of us.

The trainers, up to this point, had not show any trace fatigue, of anger, frustration or signs of being upset. They seemed to take everything in stride, unaffected by the many outbursts, questions and dramas that appeared within the space of the room. Energy seemed to be endlessly available to them as they bounded across the room dealing with each of us as we willingly grappled with experiencing issues from our past.

There were often notes passed to the trainer, causing some of us to wonder what they were about. Each time a note would be delivered to the trainer they would silently read it, seemingly discarding any sign of it having any importance. The trainer's ability to stay calm and in control became something we drew solace from as the hours dragged on.

As time passed another note came from one of the volunteers and was, as usual, presented to the trainer. He read it and then, out of character he seemed slightly ruffled. As we intensely watched this change in his demeanor, thoughts raced in as to why he was now ruffled. He again discounted his expression, saying to the assistance in the back of the room; "I will handle this."

A few minutes passed and then another note, another slight outburst from the trainer, and we watched him struggling to compose himself. A few moments passed as again his demeanor changed. He was now pissed and he expressed it vehemently. "Who in the hell was in charge of this?" No answer came forth. Shock and fear instantly burst into our minds as our experience of safety, of being lead and taught began to crumble. More drama spewed from our trainer. Right before our eyes our leader had faltered, and we began to slip into a slight state of panic, of not knowing what was happening.

We all watched as he again attempted to settle himself,

deliberately focusing, composing himself against what seemed to us as a huge problem based on his reaction. We all knew trouble was on the surface ready to erupt. We could feel it as it permeated the room. Once again, calm and collected, he began again to speak to us with a focused purpose. "Okay, I will deal with this somehow." He hollered to someone in the back of the room.

He then spoke with a tone of authority and compassion; "Ladies and gentlemen we have just been informed of a situation regarding the availability of this room. We reserved this space many months ago, yet someone has made a mistake in the schedule, the assignment of rooms. We have just been informed of a change in plans. We need to vacate this room and move this seminar to another space. This issue within itself is going to be a huge undertaking, yet the issue of a room has been solved. I also need to inform you of a bigger problem that has been brewing outside for the last 4 hours. Highway 8 has been completely closed down due to an emergency. The busses and cabs are on strike, so our normal means of travel is not an option."

Taking a breath he continued; "One of our volunteers has miraculously solved the problem of transportation, and we figured we should be able to get to Balboa Park within the hour, so here is how it lays out. This is urgent and needs to be done in an orderly manor. Get together in groups of 4. We have contacted the San Diego Zoo, and they have generously offered to send over all their elephants, donkeys, giraffes, camels, zebras, bulls and horses to supply us with transportation. Get together and into action. Decide who is going to ride which animal and write it down. When you have your lists completed give it to your group leaders. Group leaders: As soon as your lists are complete, have you people line up in lines by the volunteers who are holding signs representing your animal. Hurry, we have to be out of here in 30 minutes."

At that moment it was as though we were abandoning a sinking ship. People began to cry hysterically as others pushed and shoved, overpowering our group leader's attempts at arranging a list of the animal each of us wanted to ride on. I personally did not want to ride on the giraffe, and I let it be known with vehement force.

Now, surely you are laughing, thinking no one would fall for such a prank, such an obvious ruse, yet there was something present in that room, something often experienced in real life. It was the chaos of herd or mob rule mentality. Present in the room were, among others; lawyers, doctors, psychologists, therapists, teachers and owners of large companies. We trusted this trainer as we had been with him for about 40 hours during the past three days. His words caused us to react in a manner opposed to logic and common sense. In about 30 minutes of feverish surreal confusion we were all lined up in front of the pictures of the animals of our choices. Some of us we angry, others were frightened; tears were freely flowing as others teetered on the edges of light panic and heightened anticipation.

Then there came a loud voice of reason, of sanity, bellowing across the room. "Wake up! You are all machines being programmed by the words and actions of others."

Disbelief and shock filled the room as we slowly came to the realization of this fact sliding into our conscious minds. The trainer again barked: "Return to your seats and sit down." This was the intended point of the ruse. To wake us up, to cause awareness, the awareness of something we did not know we did not know. We were left with this following bit of wisdom.

"The only one who can be conned is someone who thinks they can not be conned." © Werner Erhard.

Chapter Thirty Three

Where is what is Missing?

There was also a statement we were left with at the end of the training. "You are whole and complete. Everything comes from language, which you have. Therefore nothing is missing."

At one point, we were asked to entertain this possibility: that we were in fact already whole and complete and that nothing was missing. As some of us mentally stepped into this possibility, a sigh of relief spilled across the room enveloping us in the comfort of those words. Then the exact quote was repeated, causing a call to action to surface as we heard that 'nothing' was missing and it needed to be found or discovered in order to be whole and complete. Such is the power of language, listening and speaking both have within them the power, the gift of choosing to view life from a new point of view...or not.

When the statement: 'nothing is missing' is heard from one point of view, it can be heard in such a way as to thwart its unbelievable value. If, using the example of 'your keys are missing,' something (your keys are missing) is heard as an action to search.

When 'nothing is missing' is heard we also can hear it as being complete within itself, like an assertion. Nothing is everywhere; therefore we are unaware of the value of the nothing that causes keys to be found. We search our memories, retrace our steps and eventually step into a new way of being called finding our keys. Something happened here that addresses the value of nothing. In the beginning we focus using our memories, recalling known places we traveled prior to misplacing our keys. As time evolves we might begin to feel a little annoyed, angry, or frustrated in the face of this unwanted situation. Then over time, again we somehow shift our focus, our thoughts, as to the seriousness of this dilemma. In the end we unconsciously shift our point of view so that we will find those keys and *poof!* the keys show up. This phenomenon manifests as unconsciously transforming the reality of not finding the keys and generating a new reality of finding our keys. In this process we unconsciously think to ourselves and finally succeed after we go through the pain or frustration of the loss of the keys.

We are unaware of transforming the 'my keys are lost conversation' or reality and generating a new 'I will find my keys' conversation or reality. This is an example of altering our way of being. If you can relate to this example you will notice that the focus and the conversation of the keys are missing gets louder and stronger as time unfolds. Now, if you experiment with this you will discover a much faster, simpler way and that is by speaking to yourself instead of thinking. A point of view causes the conversation that causes the 'way of being' which equals the results you experience. You are then at cause of creating your own 'way of being' as opposed to outside influences; panic, frustration, anger or the past of loosing your keys creating your way of thinking or being. You can speak to yourself creating your own way of 'thinking or being' into your own listening. The fun part is that you get to skip the pain and frustration.

When I did the est training one of my favorite moments was when we were given the opportunity to step into the question; "Where is what's missing?" It was presented as a game, a quandary, an invitation into the unthinkable. It was suggested to us that the value this invitation contained was accessible by learning to linger within the question. We were assured that there was tremendous value located within this quandary, and trusting the process, I chose to accept the invitation.

What I discovered was just short of miraculous. Over time I was able to grasp the possibility that 'not knowing' or 'confusion' was one of the doorways to discovery and I recognized that within myself was something that labeled confusion as either having power over me or having no meaning at all. This newly discovered part of me had a choice I was not previously aware of. In the beginning this something (confusion) came from my past programming, and it came with a meaning of something I did not want. It had meanings attached to it from my past, that of being bad or wrong, not wanted, and feeling less than or right or wrong. When it showed up when I stepped into questioning the 'confusion' it captured my attention. I noticed that confusion was in my space/context, and I just looked at it, telling it that it had no meaning, and *poof!* it vanished. I was left with a very interesting supposition: I had assumed that confusion possessed a power, a power to thwart progress, yet here I was experiencing it as powerless over the authority of my voice and my focus. In retrospect I soon discovered that my voice was spoken from the space of nothing. The space or context of who I was contained the power of a creative act prior to my machine being programmed.

One of the reasons our speaking has no control or power over our lives is that it is not our own, it is unconsciously repeated, originating from our past, not generated from our own proactive conscious choices. This way of speaking from our past is based on experiences you've had that told you that something worked or did not work to improve your life. Speaking and choosing in the present is the difference between thinking you know and knowing. Beliefs are not bad or wrong as they do have a certain amount of power, yet direct experience in a conscious moment of now has the power to alter our lives.

You might ask, how does one get direct experience as opposed to a belief? I will use a couple of personal experiences to demonstrate this. First I will present the 'past belief'. Then the 'new knowledge', state the 'how to or instructions' in two part, explain 'what happened', and then 'why' it worked:

I). The Past belief: You can't get a business license in a residential area. I had been told this was true.

*** 'The New Knowledge': Think of something you want or need. Notice what is missing. Accept the idea that everything is in constant flux or change. To acquire the experience of the something that is missing it is necessary to step out into nothing and to be in action. I knew what I wanted and I knew what was missing = a business license in a residential area.

*** First Part of the 'How to or Instructions': Go look for or ask for what is missing, knowing that the past has no meaning, no power over your request. When you look or ask, do not make the reality you encounter wrong. Do not give it meaning, it is nothing but a **trivia**.

*** First Part of what happened: At that time I lived in a residential area selling items from my house and had been previously told that I could not receive a license. I read through my notes from the est training I had attended some months ago regarding gaining experience from the knowledge of a past belief and drove to the Chamber of Commerce. I walked inside and met the person behind the counter saying; "I would like to apply for a business license." She politely handed me the form to fill out. I sat down, feeling a bit nervous; yet confident in the principle I was attempting to apply. Upon completing the form, I again approached the counter and handed it to the same woman. She looked it over and stated, in a matter of fact tone, that the street I lived on was in a residential district, and I could not receive a license to do business within that area. I thanked her for the information and returned home

The following hour I decided to take my newly gained knowledge from a past belief to a true experiment. I decided to apply for a business license.

*** Second part of the 'How to or Instructions': Repeat the first part of 'How to Instructions'. The instructions basically stated that I was to go back to the same place, speak to the same person and ask again.

*** Second Part of what happened: One hour later I went back to the same Chamber of Commerce, walked up to the same woman I had spoken to one hour prior, and again requested the form to apply for a business license. She handed it to me and I again sat down, filled out the form, returned it to the same person behind the counter. I handed it to her, and she looked it over once more and gave me the business license.

*** The Why: Simply by including the reality I experienced, being responsible for it being my past reality and not making the reality wrong, reality was transformed into me receiving what was missing.

II). The Past Belief. Reality is fixed and solid.

*** 'The New Knowledge': Think of something you want or need. Notice what is missing. Accept the idea that everything is in constant flux or change. To acquire the experience of the something that is missing it is necessary to step out into nothing and to be in action. I knew what I wanted and I knew what was missing: Money to pay the rent.

*** First part of the 'How to or Instructions': Go look for or ask for what is missing, knowing that the past has no meaning, no power over your request. When you look or ask, do not make the reality you encounter wrong. Do not give it meaning, it is nothing but a trivia.

On this particular day I decided to take my newly gained knowledge from a past belief to a true experiment: I decided to go to garage sales intending to purchase something for profit to pay the rent.

*** First part of what happened: At one of the garage sales I came across a beautiful 1920's bedroom set. It was a complete set which included a gentleman's chest of drawers, mirror, a woman's vanity along with the stool, a double bed with a pineapple four-posted headboard, footboard and two matching nightstands. During the prior year I had opened a furniture store and I desperately needed to make enough money to pay the rent, but had sadly depleted my funds to only $150.00. As I admired the bedroom set, the owner came over to me as I was expressing my appreciation for the quality of craftsmanship, beauty and design. Then she informed me of the price and I expressed to her that I thought that was very fair. We then expressed pleasantries and I left, feeling saddened by the reality. She was asking $750.00. I left thinking… if only. As I continued on in my attempts at finding something to purchase for profit, that bedroom set was never far from my thoughts. Sometime later, having found nothing to purchase, I headed back to my store still thinking about that set.

*** Second part of the 'How to or Instructions': Repeat first part of 'How to Instructions'. The instructions basically stated that I was to go back to the same place, speak to the same person and ask again.

*** Second part of what happened: I decided to swing by to see if the bedroom set had been sold, and much to my surprise it was still available. Its beauty, its craftsmanship again drew me out of my van, and I found myself once more admiring its beauty, thinking again … if only. The owner came over, recognized me from earlier and told me about her experience with regard the set. "A man came by shortly after you were here and offered me $600.00 for the set. I regret not accepting his offer, as I need to sell it today. Please make me an offer." This caught me completely off guard, as I knew I only had $150.00 to my name. I looked her straight in the eyes, pulled out my wallet and showed her all the money I had which totaled $150.00, saying I know this is not a fair offer, but it is all I have. She smiled saying; "I will take it."

I loaded it onto my van and headed back to my store, excited at the possibility of being able to sell it and pay the rent. As I pulled up in from of my store, two women who watched me load and unload furniture daily came over for a look see. Curiously they asked; "what did you find today?" I opened up my van, proud as a peacock, and showed them the beautiful bedroom set. Instantly I was pressed for a price. "I am thinking $750.00 would be a fair price." I sold it on the spot, never even having to unload it as her husband came by and picked it up about an hour later.

*** The Why: Simply by including the reality I experienced, being responsible for it being my past reality and not making the reality wrong, reality was transformed into me receiving what was missing.

Notions, thoughts, meanings, beliefs and feelings seem to fight against creating from nothing. These were all located in my past programming. One of the rewards of searching for the something that was missing and finding it was becoming privy to something unseen and unexplainable: the choice of not making the present reality wrong, the choice of learning to 'give up the right' to be stuck on the position of being right.

The choice I made was not to play the game of right and wrong, and this choice made all the difference. This presented me with the ability to transform everything that is over time.

Possessing something before you have it requires the experience of having the something before you are aware of being in the possession of it. (Recognition). It takes proactively, consciously, mentally, and as to what I state verbally reaching out (speaking your voice of authority into your own listening). (Appropriating). It is about taking hold of the past negative conversations pulling them within and embracing them rather than resisting what already is. Another way of saying this is to be responsible for what is there, and being at cause as opposed to at the effect. Responsibility meaning 'what is' minus the meanings that were attached to 'responsibility' in the past. Responsibility in not good or bad, right or wrong, better or worse, heavy, blame, burden, fault, shame or guilt. It just is, as you are context, not a thing.

"If it's never our fault, we can't take responsibility for it. If we can't take responsibility for it, we'll always be its victim." © Richard Bach.

This is a Zen principle in practice--that of not resisting. Do not make 'what is' wrong. Remember, you are practicing giving up being right. Just hear the past beliefs, meanings, thoughts and feelings as nothings, Nothing but a trivia. When one of these enters your context (the space of nothing) there will be a direct experience, an opening for you to remember your request of wanting the something, and it will come to you in time. In this example you are the Box. You and the Box will become the same with practice and patience with yourself. You will be able to transform what was (your past) into what you want, as there will be no resistance within. There is magic in this Zen principle, and through the practice of applying it you will have the experience of knowing you know it works. Verbally speaking into your own listening should be done every time in the beginning until you have a few direct experiences of your newly discovered voice of authority. It takes a shift in your consciousness to be able to recognized and apply it to overpower your past voice of past. Through time and practice, eventually you will then be able to mentally view yourself as having authority over your past meanings, the conversation, the language you allowed into your context. The Box will then become who you are, a generator and a transformer, the cause of the effect on yourself.

"At all times and under all circumstances we have the power to transform the quality of our lives." © Werner Erhard

Chapter Thirty Four

THE HOW TO: USING THE BOX

Now as to the use of this Box, follow the instructions carefully.
    Something for Nothing—A Context—a Box you choose to verbally intend to assign or create its use, its purpose. That purpose being that of putting something unwanted into it and have the meanings of this something transformed into nothing, nothing but a trivia."
     Something for Nothing. How to receive the most value from the use of the Box by applying the principles to your life.
    1) Follow the creases and fold it into the shape of a box.
    2) Consciously, proactively, choose it to be an assigned context for the something you put in it, creating it transforming into nothing, Nothing but a **trivia**.
    3) Place the box somewhere in your living space. Consciously, proactively (speak your words into your own listening). "This Box is a context, and I intend to assign or create its use, its purpose. That purpose being that of putting something within it and have the meanings of this something transformed into nothing, Nothing but **a trivia**."
    I call this: 'putting it (the **Box**) there' on purpose.
    *** Causing or choosing it to be where it is and what it is. "I choose to give this Box a purpose. As I put something into it, this thing's meanings transform or disappear into nothing, Nothing but a **trivia**."
    Next to your bed is optimal if you have trouble getting a good night sleep if you have a chattering mind. Do whatever works for you.

4) Ask yourself this question, and give yourself a chance to succeed with this:

"What meaning, feeling, belief, issue or annoying thought would I be willing to let go of and cause it to turn into Nothing but a trivia, transform--disappear?" Or at the least, diminish in its size of importance, meaning or power over my life?

5) Write this meaning, feeling, belief, issue or annoying thought on a piece of paper, fold it up and consciously, proactively insert it into the box saying, "I consciously, proactively put you here. I am removing you from my space. You are nothing. You are Nothing but a trivia. You no longer have any meaning or power over me."

Remember, you are using your voice to override, overpower, replace, manage and direct something that you have allowed to sneak into your space/context making you believe that it has power over you. Remember logic and common sense. Remember the height and weight example. We are taller than and weigh more than a meaning, a thought, a feeling, a belief, or an issue.

6) As you begin to fall asleep, your meaning, belief, thought or feeling might attempt to escape from the Box by coming back into the context of your mind or body. Continue to put them back inside the Box with your voice (in the beginning) or thinking the thoughts: "Get back in that box where I designated you to stay. You have no power over me. You are Nothing but a trivia." Again, speaking it is optimal in the beginning. Do NOT make it wrong, ask it, beg it or plead with it. Firmly demand it by using the gift you are learning to use correctly--your voice of authority. Assert yourself. It is just a lazy muscle. Use it until it gets back in shape. This takes a little time and practice.

Over time you will experience an identity shift within your voice, not a crisis, remember? At first this shift will be very subtle. Just notice it and remember the part of your mind of past that once controlled you is still wanting to override your voice. This past in love with attention and control will want you to forget so just thank it for sharing. If doubting the workability of this practice shows up, place that doubt in the Box, also telling it that it is nothing, Nothing but a trivia.

7) Use power, not force. Let me explain. True power is drawn from within. You are just not aware of the power you already have—yet. When you begin to correctly apply what you have learned you can remove something from your context by recognizing it as something you unknowingly allowed into your space, something {language} you allowed to have power over you. You now know how to deal with it from the point of authority. You have a choice to deal with it once and for all. Do it until you experience that power coming from within. It is there, trust me, I know as I suffered being powerless for far too long. Remember, it is like a muscle. When it has not been used it goes into atrophy, getting lazy and lacking power. Force is used to get something that belongs to another for yourself. Don't waste your efforts.

"Force always attracts men of low morality." © Albert Einstein

8) 'Putting it there' requires some explanation. When you put something inside the Box, it goes in as something and in time comes out as nothing, or transforms into nothing: a trivia, so to speak. Here is the tricky, yet amazing part. When something is within your context, the something (thought) you relate to, or has your attention--argue with, fight, dodge, get frustrated with, ignore, get angry at, resist, plead with to go away, have tried to fix, disagreed with, hated, it is upsetting you. It is something you have been told to give meaning to. You did not choose the meanings. The meanings were there prior to your birth. The big, smart, expert, cleaver, creative, strong, important people told you the meanings. You did not choose. When you place something inside the Box, it is transformed into nothing, a trivia or lack of meaning or power, based on you having designated the Box to be used for this purpose. What will disappear is the meaning you were told had power over you. Remove the meaning, and its power over you is also removed. You now have a say, via your consciously proactively spoken voice in the matters of your life. You are creating speaking, versus speaking creating you and speaking into your own listening versus the voices of past programming talking to you. You are at Cause vs. at the Effect.

Proactive vs, Reactive. In Control vs. being Controlled. Powerful vs. powerless. Victor vs. Victim.

9) The amazing part of this process is that once you have created a void by making something transform or disappear, there is now space for something new. There is a postulate attributed to Aristotle stating that nature abhors a void. This space now contains a void you have created, and you can choose what you would prefer to fill this space. This is where being alert becomes of great importance. Until you learn to choose for yourself the past habit of not proactively, consciously choosing will automatically step up to fill this space. It takes alertness, time, patience and practice to become accustomed to having a voice of authority, a choice with power over your past. The past thing, issue, circumstance, belief, habit, thought or meaning will not have any meanings attached to it--or no power, yet it will want to regain control and reinsert its power and meaning over you. It is as though the past continually wants to test you, making sure you truly have established a firm grasp on being at cause, as the mind of past fears change and the loss of its control and power.

Once you have gained some direct experiences of power over your past you will become consciously aware of this power within. Once this awareness in attained something special becomes available. I like to call this character with power my 'looker'. The 'looker' resides at the very core of our being. It hears all, sees all, is patient, mostly forgiving and able to tolerate…up to a point. It is a feeling of resolve, a line of demarcation, a line in the sand or a boundary. When this point is reached, the choice to bend no further and draw on its limitless power becomes available. Some call this sick and tired of being sick and tired. Others might relate to this as enough is enough.

Remember we spoke about the power of this word 'enough' earlier as not being something outside of yourself. This character I call my 'looker', my voice, speaks 'enough' into existence, taping that power of resolve, not having to wait until something outside of me causes me to respond. I create the power of 'enough' appearing from nothing by speaking it to my own listening. I generate it.

It is of this power that I speak of here. After you have

practiced and applied these principles to your own life, and experienced the subtle shift in your way of being, you will be able to simply mentally 'look' directly at a thought, meaning, feeling, belief or issue. You will be able to mentally generate (cause thinking) and address something unwanted with authority and repeat; "You are nothing but a trivia hanging out rent free inside my space or context. Get out of here! I will do the choosing as to who controls my life." Over time 'it' will give up, as it can't handle being seen (perceived) as being nothing but a **trivia**. It will eventually shrivel and shrink from your consciousness.

After more practice and application, you will be able to transform a thing, issue, meaning, feeling, belief or issue that somehow secretly sneaked into your space or context without using the Box. Just stop, look within and listen. Take a few moments to identify the culprit within your space or context, the feeling, the meaning, belief or issue and address it with authority.

Once it is specifically recognized, you can now begin to call upon your power, applying it with the focus of intense purpose, that being of placing the thing, the meaning, belief, feeling, or issue outside of your space or context by speaking our loud. "I put you out there, I see you out there." Just see some object or space outside of yourself and tell whatever snuck into your space that it is out there, and not in your space. Speaking into your own listening with authority will eventually cause you to believe it and then much to your amazement you will 'experience' it leaving your space. In that moment you will have **experienced** the **something** that is more valuable than understanding, your own true voice of power, untarnished by your past.

10) After discovering this gift I came across a few more things I began to say to myself that turned out to be very powerful if my life began to go awry: "This is not the way God, Budda or Spirit intended me to be. I have thoughts, thoughts do not have me. I somehow allowed you into my space and I can choose to remove you. I choose to live my life being at cause, not at the effect. I have within myself everything needed to handle this. Self-leadership and self control was a gift given to

me and I mistakenly allowed others to take it from me. I am willing to be taught even when I resist the teaching. My worth is a given as opposed to having to earn it. Asking for help is a sign of strength. That door to experience is never locked because I have the only key, though knocking and asking are highly recommended. From moments of direct experience comes something greater than understanding. Thoughts are like barking stray dogs, therefore I can choose which ones to feed. Birds like thoughts, come and go. I can choose which ones I allow to make a nest."

11) After all this is said and done, here is the part for those who want to live on this planet in a peace beyond understanding. Over time, practice consciously proactively choose to alter your point of view, choose to have everyone on the planet be perfect just the way they are--and the way they are not. At that point you can do the same thing with everything else on the planet. Simply have it be the way it is and the way it is not. Guess what? " It is the way it ... and it is the way it is not." © Werner Erhard. Judgment is transformed into Discernment.

"It is better to conquer yourself than to win a thousand battles. Then the victory is yours. It cannot be taken from you, not by angels or by demons, heaven or hell." © Buddha

P. S. You are now enlightened.

Chapter Thirty Five

A Few Bonuses

The Games of Empowerment

Compliments, when accepted, have the potential of raising our self worth, our value and our mood, therefore putting a smile on both the giver and the receiver's faces. However, when compliments are rejected, there is another dynamic present. The cause of this dynamic that thwarts this potential gift from being received is the chatter of the programmed mind of the past. The meanings we have given to receiving 'something for nothing' may be positive or negative based on your past experience. To say that there is no such thing as something for nothing sets up an unconscious barrier between you receiving these free uplifting gifts. Society has used this phrase to cause us to place walls between us and ourselves, causing us to assume that we have to protect ourselves from everything. What go unnoticed are the costs of us thwarting these gifts of receiving. First of all, when the person gives a compliment, usually his or her intent is to make someone feel good. Secondly their intent is to cause good feelings within themselves. Seldom does this dynamic get completed if the receiver is unable to get past their mind and receive the gift. There is a conversation of expectation running amuck, as both the giver and the receiver unconsciously believe that there is a cost.

To be sure there are a few people who do not expect something when they give a gift, yet it is the exception not the rule. We often respond or react as if it is the rule. So too often, the giver is left with rejection and the receiver is left silently complaining about not receiving what they need now and then. This is not a mystery. We all need to be complimented and encouraged throughout out lives. This dynamic is that it comes from being programmed to protect you from the language that we are so often being bombarded with. This unconscious response reaction has become a costly habit, unseen as to both its cause and its effect. The solution is to simply say the words 'thank you', disregarding the mind of past with all its chatter about whether or not you deserve it. What you will have done is a step toward cracking open the door to receiving, a perfect example of letting go of being right. Over time you will feel your self worth subtly returning.

"I can live for two months on a good compliment." © Mark Twain

As I mentioned earlier there is a game two people can play that creates the magic of transformation. This game is one of those activities in which you can manifest something extremely valuable from nothing that costs you nothing. You simply recognize your voice and appropriate it. It's that easy: notice something you are having trouble creating or something you are having trouble getting rid of. Simply create a game with someone you trust, create rules to the game that support both of you winning and then stick to them.

Say you are having trouble getting rid of a belief: "My life is boring". (Your point of view about your life). Your partner hears and sees this from a different point of view.

The rules to the game.

A. The agreements of the person who sees their life as being boring.

1) I agree to give up my position of being right (my point of view).

2) I agree to allow my partner to be right, expressing "you are right" and not make their point of view wrong. (Managing the mind of past responses).

3) I agree to say 'thank you' every time they offer their point of view, even when I do not agree with them or believe it.

4) I agree to play this game with full abandonment, with gusto and excitement.

5) I agree to play this game for ten minutes with my partner every day until I experience a shift in my point of view, my past belief.

B. The part of the coach.

1) Agree to listen to their partner's point of view, their belief.
2) I agree not to make their point of view wrong. I will say: "I got it". = (You are not attached to the meanings of having a headache).
3) Verbally replace their belief of; "My life is boring" with; "You have an exciting life." Pointing out the moments and memories you see as exciting in the person's life. Compliment them for sharing exciting stories and memories, expressing how much value it adds to people's lives and yours. Remember, they cannot see what you see, so be patient.
4) Now, just have your normal conversations with your friend asking them to continue to express their point of view. Each time they express that their life is boring, do not make it wrong. Just offer your point of view again. You might occasionally be required to remind them of the rules of the game they agreed to play.

The results will totally amaze you. This is the shortest, easiest, most direct way to reach the subconscious mind.

In the beginning of the game, the two most difficult parts of the process are the letting go of being right (their point of view) and allowing another's point of view to influence them. Over time and a few direct experiences of playing this game, you will be able to do this at will and the Box will not be necessary. The Box is simply a representation of who you are and what you are capable of. A context with made up meanings from the past.

"To keep a person from discovering their true self, convince them that they can not makes thinks disappear." © Werner Erhard. This may not be the exact quote, but it is close enough.

It is similar to having a coach who can see your blind spots. As they are listening and observing you, they are looking from a different point of view. Their view is from outside of the subjugated box you are stuck in and they can see and hear what is in your context, your blind spots clearly. The coach's goal it to make you better, to support you receiving what you say you want. Your part is to trust the process, their guidance, insights and experiences causing you to receive what you want. This is a win---win game.

When two people play the game of being a coach for each other, both people win, as each experience giving and receiving. There is a name for this kind of relationship. It is called a relationship based on **feed not need or a power-fed relationship**. It takes the mind in love with attention and control out of its power position.

If sleeplessness is an issue you want to transform, there is a very simple solution. Verbally (speak it into your own listening) designate (assign the purpose of) your bed as a space or context for sleeping, sex or listening to the pitter-patter of the rain. Listen to your thoughts, the mental chatter that is running around in your head when you sink your head into the pillow. Pick a thought or belief that you have allowed into the designated space of your bed. Pick one that does not support the context of the bed, your desire to sleep. Get up and write it down, write it down and insert it into the Box that you assigned for the purpose of transforming something into nothing, Nothing but a trivia. Use your newly discovered voice of authority and choose to designate this thought to become nothing, Nothing but a trivia. You are now speaking to your thoughts from your point of view—the point where you now have power over the voices from the past. How long will it take to get the results I say are there? Do it until it happens, meaning do it until you 'experience' the thought, belief, meaning, feeling or issue diminishes.

Once you step into this experience, your will never be the same person, as you will have experienced the true power the something you allowed others to take from you. The alternative is, as I have stated prior, you will be left with being stuck on the position of being right and I will be left with this Book and a Box adding zero value to your life.

By the time you finish reading this book you will understand why sleeplessness among other things, is an epidemic running rapid, requiring a plethora of drugs to be taken, in an attempt to solve the problem. Most of this is totally unnecessary and a waste of time and money.

Also, with regard to the issue of sleeplessness, here is

another possible solution, a little gem I picked up along the way. It has a twinge of a spiritual flair to it, but it is not religious in nature, so give it a chance to work.

Every house is different, so work with me. When you lay your head on the pillow and close your eyes, follow these directions:

* Starting with the pillow covers, 'mentally' with thought only, bless each of them.
* Bless each pillowslip and then bless the pillow.
* Now, in your mind, with (thoughts), start from one side of your bedroom and think or picture each and every object in your bedroom and bless it, continuing around the bedroom.
* Now bless the door out of your bedroom and enter the next room.
* Bless every item as you mentally walk through your residence.
* In the bathroom, bless the sink, the shower, the tub, the toilet, the towels, the wastebasket, etc.
* Now the next room, next room. In the kitchen bless the refrigerator the stove and so on until you reach the front door.
* If you have a back door bless it as you pass it by.
* If you are not asleep by now, mentally step outside and bless your residence. Actually see if you can view your residence with a thought or a picture, just for a second.
* Then if necessary mentally bless the neighborhood you live in, always by viewing it with your mind.
* If you are still awake, bless the town, then the state, then bless any states you have visited. Bless any state you can picture or think about.
* If you are still awake, bless the USA from afar, and now bless the earth from above.

The point of this amazing solution to the issue of sleeplessness is that each time you encounter mentally focusing on blessing each item, you are pressing up against your unconscious, which will put you to sleep. You are training or using your mind to think thoughts that have nothing to do with meanings attached to not sleeping. Again we have this premise; no two things can occupy the same space. You are proactively and consciously causing or placing thoughts into your context about blessing this and that, replacing the thoughts of not being able to sleep. You are training or using your mind to think of something other than thinking about not sleeping or not thinking about not sleeping. The spiritual aspect of this is that as you get closer to blessing the USA or the earth, you are getting closer to nothingness, where sleeplessness is no longer.

Headaches are another very interesting issue, which is addressed with the saying that no two things can occupy the same space. If a headache comes from thoughts of stress or worry there is a very simple way to transform or clear most headaches. It is a little demonstration I was privy to during the est training I attended in the early 70's and it can be easily accomplished simply with the power within the spoken language.

Example: Have the person with the headache sit comfortably in a chair with you sitting opposite them. Ask them this question: "Is this okay with you and would you be willing to have your headache disappear without understanding how it is done?" When you receive a yes, continue on to the next part. Explain that you are going to ask them to do this with their eyes closed, as it will assist them in focusing clearly. Let then know you are going to ask a series of questions regarding the headache's 'specific' location—for example, three inches above my right ear and ½" inside my skin. Now, what shape is it? What color is it? Is it hard? Soft? What is its volume? As in, how much liquid would it hold? A pint, cup, quart or teaspoon? Explain to them that when you ask these questions you want them to answer from present time, not the past. This is very important.

Begin to ask any of these following questions in any order slowly at first, then in a semi rapid cadence, and just listen for any conversations that may come from their past. The order in which you ask the questions does not matter, yet I usually start with the location. Believe me, you will know when they are answering from the past.

"Where is it located now?" Wait for a 'specific' response.
"What color is it now?" Wait for a response.
"How much liquid would it hold?" Wait for a response.
"What shape is it? Wait for a response.
"Is it hard or soft? Wait for a response.

"Where is it located now?" Wait for a 'specific' response.
"What shape is it? Wait for a response.
"How much liquid would it hold?" Wait for a response, and so on.

When you hear them repeat their answers from their past just kindly remind them to answer the question **from now, not the past.** You will easily get a sense of them answering from their past after a few questions as you will hear the same answer being repeated. Don't make the response wrong: just remind them to answer from **right now.** Remember the mind of past in love with attention and control is still present as most people are not accustomed to answering questions in present time as the are stuck in the past of having the headache.

As you go through a few rounds of asking these questions at random and hearing their answers, you will be able to notice a shift in the specific location, color change, softness or hardness answer, shape of, or amount of liquid contained.

It is a little like coaching someone toward having no headache. Stay focused on them, looking at where they say their headache is located and listening to what they say about their headache. Remember we all have a looker. As the coach you are listening from the part of you that is looking from your point of view, silently yet truthfully you are transforming the meanings and feelings attached to the headache into trivia as you do not have the headache. As they are answering your questions they are unaware of detaching from the meanings from the headache. You are outside of their context looking in, assisting in the causing of it disappearing.

As you continue to ask the questions, you are listening for clues such as the color changing, the shape altering, the size changing; the specific location shifting. Just tell your subject what you see and hear them saying, that the headache is in the process of moving around, changing colors, location and shapes. That is real progress. Usually within five or ten minutes you will notice them searching for the color, shape, size or specific location and you will soon get a sense of it being gone. Just ask them, where is it right now? You might remind them of their agreement to have it disappear and not understand it. Allow them to discover not being able to locate it. If the headache is still there continue on, repeating the process. This like any new ability it takes a few practice sessions, but over time you will become proficient at it. I have actually done this on myself, but it is a bit more difficult to coach myself. Remember, understanding is the booby prise, so if the person gets rid of the headache and it then comes back, they tried to understand the process you both just went through. You coached them in stepping away from the mind in love with attention and control and they looked back at the headache and made it dissappear. Kind of like a miracle!

There once was a seed that grew into a mighty tree. From the tree someone formed something--an idea called paper. Over time that idea of paper was formed into cardboard. A thought form would be a good name for it. This Box is just cardboard folded up, and then thought formed into a Box. Then this Box was thought formed again by adding some color, and then thought formed again by the addition of a verse; a context or purpose, and then *Poof*! We now have something that was thought formed into something that could be seen as having more value than it had as a piece of paper—or just maybe a mighty tree.

Now, I will surmise that we all understand this principle of progress or the evolution of ideas.

The question I would like to pose for you to consider is this; **What was there prior to the seed?**

"To know, is to know that you know nothing. That is the meaning of true knowledge." © Socrates

The End

This book was written for education and the pleasure of writing it.

And as it was so brilliantly stated in Richard Bach's book Illusions, "Everything in this book may be wrong."

as it is simply written from my point of view.

All Knowledge is Divided into Three domains:

"What We Know", "What We Know That We Don't Know" and "What We Don't Know That We Don't Know."
© Werner Erhard

The Author

Vic Van Maren Jr. has 43 years experience as a Landmark Forum/EST. {Erhard Seminars Training} graduate. Through the creative use of language that experience is reflected in his books. His previous publications include: three Magicardstories™: "The Wizard of Wishes.", "Little Joe and the Joker." and "The Wizard of Possibility".

The author is currently retired, enjoys writing & selling on Ebay, Bonanza and Facebook and lives in La Mesa, CA.

A Magicardstory ™ is a story, told by you and a deck of playing cards. Even though you have someone cut the cards 5 different times, the cards match the story as it unfolds, creating a .... MAGICAL ILLUSION of the cards APPEARING .... AS YOU SPEAK! All three of the Magicardstories™ work the same way, however the story you tell is different.

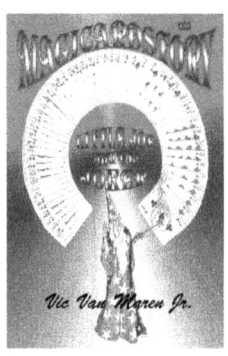  

Also **"Victims of the Voice. The Audacity of an Idea"**

It is a story about Izy, an audacious idea whose time has come. It is a parable, about the search and discovery of a secret treasure of tremendous power. It is a gift given to each and every person at birth and is hidden in plain sight. When it is used it multiplies, having the immense power of disappearance and manifestation. It is infinite. It contains nothing and everything, containing no past and no future. It is free, acquired by recognition and appropriation.

Also: **"Secret Whispers of the Wind"**

The true story of my experiences of going through a divorce, seeking help, meeting unbelievable people on my road to recover and then following three gals along the freeway one night, who introduced me to an educational program called the Landmark Forum. After going through the training, I was able to create winning an 8-day, all expense paid trip to St. Lucia in the Caribbean Islands.

As we departed and as the plane left the ground, Kelly, the man I chose to take with me, began to open me up to a world I knew very little about. As I spoke, he listened. Then he spoke and I listened. It was then, in that moment that I began to experienced unbelievable power, emotional overload and feelings that had been hidden in the darkness of the fears of my past, the limits of my mind. They were spoken by a man I came to know and love, as he secretly waved his magic wand and those fears disappeared into the nothingness of my mind.

As we flew over Florida he quietly asked what I wished to experience on the Island. I began to babble, as those wishes that had been conceived in the painful experiences of the divorce, bubbled forth. I felt the same safety in expressing those wishes as I experienced with Jackie, a dear friend in San Diego who had opened my mind and heart to the many breathtaking moments of beauty and of learning.

I was to experience deja vu, having the Midas touch and I was to find women by feeling the energy of her spirit, using only this newly discovered intuition. I experienced floating on the consolations of her thoughts, giving her a magical star, experienced both of our wishes come true as we were being teleported into passages in books we had both read. I had thoughts materialize moment to moment, allowing the power of destiny to gently draw us both into the melding of our thoughts, then into a vortex absence of time and space, a space beyond our knowing. At least ten of the outrageous wishes I had expressed to Kelly on the plane came true in the space of those 8 days.

We both experienced the playful creative innocence of a child as we stepped briefly into Kelly's world. Katherine was then picked up by a chariot, became a princess royally welcomed as we arrived at the ball. Then she floated on that playfulness as I told her of the gift she was about to win. I knew, but knew not how I knew she was about to win.

Also: "The Money Game. How to Make Money Work for you."

Working hard for your Money is a subconscious choice we all make, thinking it is our only choice, based on our beliefs, experiences, programing and surroundings. This book is about choosing to alter that choice, at first based on simply trusting that it is possible. It is like choosing an ice cream flavor, not ever having tasted the flavor chosen. Once chosen, the risk is in trusting the unlimited experiences of someone who has done it for 36 years. Over time you will begin learning and discover freedom from that daily grind and step into the world of unlimited financial possibilities. I quit my job in 1977.

The cost is the price of this book and being willing to hold at bay the chatter of your mind telling you it will not work. For each of you it will take a different amount of time to "see the light" as something other than a train coming at you full speed. This light is actually freedom from the pressure of preforming for another and receiving only the scraps from the financial table of life. We all want financial freedom, the freedom to enjoy five days and only work the other two.   Well, it is possible and if you are willing to learn, I will take you step by step through the pitfalls and share with you the rewards of being an entrepreneur. I didn't have a teacher, so I gutted it out, learning these profitable lessons on the schoolyard of hard knocks.

Seeing huge % profit returns and cashing in on them opened my eyes to a world beyond my past beliefs of what was possible and is available to anyone who was willing to take the risk.

Not having to quit your day job until you know it is the right thing to do is paramount to your success. The huge rewards outweigh the risk 10-1 and the education you will receive investing in yourself will become invaluable as you experience it unfold in your daily life.

You can go anywhere and cash in on profit$ you see, making life a joyous adventure and an education combined into one. Money is everywhere, yet it is hidden in plain sight, waiting for you to learn to see it, pick it up, mentally reframe it and put the **PROFIT** in your pocket.

**WOOPIE!
PARADIGM SHIFT!**

To Order Your Own Paperback Copy of any of these books go to: **thebookpatch.com**, **Amazon.com** or **barnesandnoble.com** For **E-Books go to Amazon.com.** Just type in my name and all the books I have written will come up.

□ □ □

www.ingramcontent.com/pod-product-compliance
Lightning Source LLC
Chambersburg PA
CBHW061256110426
42742CB00012BA/1943